CHOOSE THE LIFE

EXPLORING

a FAITH

That

EMBRACES

DISCIPLESHIP

Bill Hull

BakerBooks
Grand Rapids, Michigan

© 2004 by Bill Hull

Published by Baker Books
a division of Baker Book House Company
P.O. Box 6287, Grand Rapids, MI 49516-6287
www.bakerbooks.com

Printed in the United States of America

Library of Congress Cataloging-in-Publication Data
Hull, Bill, 1946–
    Choose the life : exploring a faith that embraces discipleship / Bill Hull.
        p.   cm.
    ISBN 0-8010-6470-8 (pbk.)
    1. Christian life. I. Title.
    BV4501.3.H845 2004
    248.4—dc22   2003027994

Illustrations are from Bill Thrall, Bruce McNicol, and Ken McElrath, *The Ascent of a Leader* (San Francisco: Jossey-Bass, 1999). Copyright © 1999. Reprinted by permission of John Wiley & Sons, Inc.

"In a churchly culture of many decisions but few disciples, Bill Hull challenges us to exchange ingrained patterns of unfruitful mediocrity for the paradigm of radically following Jesus on the path of transformational discipleship. If faithfully heeded, *Choose the Life* will revolutionize the people of God."

—Bruce Demarest, professor of Christian theology and spiritual transformation, Denver Seminary

"Hull, I believe, correctly identifies that though there is a growing concern among some evangelicals about the lack of true spiritual formation, this is a problem of a more fundamental nature that has been with many of us for much longer than many of us realize, namely, a vapid version of the gospel. He makes a compelling and inarguable case that the cross of Christ requires us to restore the crucial dimension of discipleship—a long obedience in the footsteps of Jesus—to our proclamations and invitations. I couldn't agree with him more. Until we make the crucial correction, it's useless to think we can expect our people to get excited about things like serving the overlooked or racial reconciliation."

—Ken Fong, senior pastor, Evergreen Baptist Church, Los Angeles

"Bill Hull's *Choose the Life* is a wonderful book for those tired of ho-hum Christianity. He gets right to the heart of what being a disciple of Jesus Christ means. With the drastic drop of the number of evangelicals in the last ten years, he sounds a wakeup call for the church and addresses some of the reasons for this from both a biblical perspective and his very personal account of God's work in his own life."

—Clyde Cook, president, Biola University

"It is a joy to commend this book to all Christians, and to all who want to learn what Christianity really is whether you are a believer or not. Bill Hull has genuinely revealed his soul and his experience as a pastoral leader, but more than that, he has gotten to the heart of things in a rare way."

—Richard E. Averbeck, professor of Old Testament and Semitic languages, Trinity Evangelical Divinity School

"In a fresh new way Bill challenges us to look again at the mandate to 'make disciples of all nations.' This book will challenge you, refresh you, and stir the passions of your life to the greatest of all causes—Great Commission living."

—Dann Spader, founder and executive director, Sonlife Ministries

Other Titles by Bill Hull

CONTENTS

FOREWORD

There are now signs that significant groups among professing Christians are ready to take up discipleship to Jesus as the core of their religious life. A realization has been setting in that the redemption Christ offers is for all aspects of life, from the deepest parts of the human being outward to the last details of our actions. Many who previously had only a superficial connection with Christ are coming to understand that whole-life discipleship to him is the easy way to live: the "easy yoke" and the "light burden" that Jesus promised to those who step into the yoke with him to learn of him.

We will see great progress for Jesus' work on earth, and great blessing upon the lives of groups and individuals, if this new seriousness about discipleship stays focused on three things.

First, there must be no mistaking the fact that discipleship to Jesus means primarily learning from him how to do—easily and routinely do—the very things he said for us to do. Obedience is the only sound objective of a Christian spirituality. Of course, we do not obey to earn anything—earning is out of the question—but we obey because doing the things that Jesus said is what is best for us and for everyone around us.

Second, we do not become able to obey by trying to obey, but by becoming the kind of person who naturally does obey. That means our intention is to acquire, by intelligent effort and grace, the inward character of Jesus Christ himself. We think and feel like him; our will has his habits of choosing; our very body is poised toward righteous deeds; and our way of relating to others is governed by his kind of love.

Third, the activities of our fellowship groups and their leaders are explicitly designed to make disciples—not some lesser version of "Christian," but genuine apprentices to Jesus in kingdom living—and to teach everyone in the group to do the things Jesus said. Leaders do this by bringing their fellowship groups through effective processes of inward transformation of the dynamics of human life.

In this way we will do what Jesus told us to do: "Make disciples as you go, submerge them in the Trinitarian reality, and train them to do everything that I commanded you" (paraphrase of Matt. 28:19–20). That is what it means to choose the life. The ills of the church and of the individual derive almost totally from the simple failure to do what Jesus told us to do in the Great Commission. There is no excuse whatsoever for not doing it, and every rationalization is simply a wound to our own souls, an injury to our groups, and an insult to the Christ who told us what to do.

Bill Hull has learned a lot from his years in the church as a pastor and leader. Most importantly, as this book shows, he has learned about himself. He has a vivid sense that what matters is what you are on the inside; that is the place where discipleship takes hold and where the only possible foundation for uncomplicated obedience is laid. He is delightfully candid and fresh, and conveys profound substance with stark clarity. You will wince as he relates painful experiences incurred while trying to lead his church to "great things" with thoughts and feelings remaining un-Christlike. But you will see with joy how character—not just bright ideas and slick techniques—has genuine power in human relationships under God.

He has found that "an environment of grace is a community in which disciples accept each person where they are, celebrate how God has made them, and encourage each other to train to be godly." We can only hope and pray that the desire to build such communities will now become widely contagious, as has been gloriously so in past times among Jesus' people.

Dallas Willard

PREFACE
A Conversation Starter

When I read a book, I like to know what the basic issues are in a nutshell. In this preface I'll lay some important groundwork for the reader to have in mind as the book is read. I see a problem in the health of the church that is connected to our inability to be what we advertise ourselves to be. This, then, explains our inability to affect others and fulfill the Great Commission. We live in a world where 95 percent of preaching is directed to 6 percent of the Western world's population, yet the church is shrinking. Therefore, I will offer a summary of the problem and the solution.

I hope the talking points that follow this summary will generate conversation among readers. The remainder of the book explores the kind of life that Jesus called us to—a life in a different realm, in his kingdom, if you will. In this kingdom he leads and we follow; his will is done in our lives and in those we affect.

The book's title speaks of making a choice, namely, to *choose the life* that Christ calls us to—a special kind of life that only disciples can embrace, a life that Dietrich Bonhoeffer described so well as a life of "costly grace" rather than "cheap grace." "We Lutherans," Bonhoeffer wrote, "have gathered like eagles round the carcase of cheap grace, and there we have drunk of the poison which has killed the life of following Jesus."[1] The cost of discipleship is our willingness to leave all things behind and follow Jesus wherever he leads. Cheap grace is the bitterest foe of discipleship, which true discipleship must loathe and detest. It is our enemy because it makes a life of transformation optional. "We must never make cheap what was costly to God,"[2] said Bonhoeffer. The problem stated below explains how we have cheapened grace.

You will notice the book's subtitle speaks of "exploring a faith that embraces discipleship." I have used "exploring a faith" because I would like for you to reconsider what we mean by faith. A faith that separates salvation from discipleship is not the faith of the New Testament. Faith without obedience is not real; it is nothing more than an intellectual exercise. The faith taught to us by Jesus embraces a lifelong abandonment of following Jesus whatever the cost or destination.

You might wonder why I have used "discipleship" instead of the currently popular term "spiritual formation." I cast my lot with John Stott on this matter. "I've never liked very much the phrase spiritual formation," Stott said to an American interviewer, "any more than I like the word spirituality. They seem to perpetuate the disastrous division between spiritual and secular. . . . The second reason I don't like it is because it's not really a biblical phrase. The biblical phrase for spirituality and spiritual formation is discipleship."[3]

1. Dietrich Bonhoeffer, *The Cost of Discipleship* (New York: Macmillan, 1949), 57–58.
2. Ibid., 48.
3. Timothy Dudley-Smith, *John Stott: A Biography: The Later Years* (Downers Grove, Ill.: InterVarsity, 2001), 451.

THE PROBLEM OF AND SOLUTION TO A NONDISCIPLESHIP CHRISTIANITY

The Problem

Dietrich Bonhoeffer said, "Christianity without discipleship is always Christianity without Christ."[4] Enough of the church has accepted a nondiscipleship Christianity to render it ineffective at its primary task—the transformation of individuals and communities into the image of Christ. This Christless Christianity has created leaders who are addicted to recognition and success and congregations that believe forsaking all things to follow Jesus is optional and a separate issue from salvation.

Too many have been taught that faith means to agree to a set of religious facts about Jesus rather than choosing to take up their cross daily and follow him. This shredding of justification from sanctification has done great damage to the authenticity and power of the gospel. It has created a church where faith equals intellectual assent, and high commitment is the exception rather than the norm. Therefore, in the United States, the church continues to shrink in size, lacks relevancy because of moral duplicity, and preaches a gospel that produces more consumers of religious goods and services than disciples.

The Solution

What is needed is a new hermeneutic, one that is as old as the New Testament itself. There is widespread confusion about the nature of salvation because of the separation of justification from sanctification. The gospel we preach must make whole again the unity of justification and sanctification. Bonhoeffer does this with his statement that "only the believer is obedient—only the obedient believe."[5] Justification and sanctification can be unified within the single concept of discipleship.

4. Bonhoeffer, Cost of Discipleship, 67.
5. Eberhard Bethge, Dietrich Bonhoeffer: A Biography (Minneapolis: Fortress, 2000), 450.

Justification is the new creation of the new person, and sanctification is the preservation, protection, and the development of that person until the day of Jesus Christ. The moment the believer repents of his sin and answers the call of Jesus in "If anyone would come after me, he must deny himself and take up his cross daily and follow me" (Luke 9:23), he is justified; he steps into a new and special life. The act of faith that justifies is also the engine of sanctification; both are unified in discipleship, the lifelong journey of following and obeying Jesus.

Ours is a gospel that calls every person to believe what Jesus believed, live as he lived, love as he loved, serve as he served, and lead as he led. It has the power to revolutionize the meaning of faith and restore to the church its growth, morality, and ability to influence an increasingly skeptical and needy world.

To summarize what is wrong with the gospel we preach,

- it is truncated, limiting grace to forgiveness of sins
- it separates justification from sanctification
- it teaches that faith equals agreement with a set of facts
- it allows discipleship to be optional
- it does not require cross bearing and thus allows for cheap grace[6]
- it does not require repentance

Now is the time for us to turn the corner and reject this false gospel.

- We must proclaim a more complete gospel that unifies justification and sanctification under the rubric of discipleship. When by God's grace we are enabled to repent of our sin, we choose to enter into a new realm of his kingdom. It is a call to a life, a journey of following Jesus.

6. Cheap grace is when we cheapen what was costly to God. When our response to God's costly sacrifice is not discipleship, we have made his gift cheap.

- We must create environments of grace where principles of grace are lived out.[7] This is because we lack a practical theology of grace.
- We must teach the proper use of the spiritual disciplines. The disciplines are a response to God's grace, enabled by his grace, in order to position ourselves for transformation.
- We must teach believers to be disciples and to make disciples among the lost and broken.
- We must help believers deal with "below the line" issues—the "show stoppers" that block transformation.
- We must understand that the above, when lived out, will create a kingdom influence.[8]

TALKING POINTS

Change "The Ask"

The way we do evangelism needs to include an invitation to life as a seamless whole that begins now and stretches into the eternal state. In other words, we need to change "the ask." Our invitation needs to start with repentance and unify justification and sanctification under the rubric of discipleship. A gospel that makes disciples is one where faith is real only when there is obedience.

7. Grace (from *charis*) is a gift. It is a means to obtaining something we can't earn or lack the capacity to achieve. "For by grace you have been saved through faith—and this is not from yourselves, it is a gift of God—not by works so that no one can boast," and this grace extends to all spiritual activity for all our lives: "For we are God's workmanship, created in Christ Jesus to do good works, which God prepared in advance for us to do" (Eph. 2:8–10). Grace, then, is God's continued gift of his enablement. The divine ability to do good works, to give a great effort, is all a part of his grace: "Continue to work out your salvation with fear and trembling, for it is God who works in you *to will* and *to act* according to his good purpose" (Phil. 2:12b–13, emphasis mine).

8. The original thinking concerning what is wrong with the gospel we preach came in a conversation with five friends who are a part of TACT (Theological and Cultural Thinkers), a group committed to thinking and writing about spiritual transformation and discipleship.

Becoming Gently Intolerant of Fringe Christianity

The church needs discipleship evangelism—evangelizing the church to choose the life of discipleship—but the church struggles with what it means to follow Jesus. This book, therefore, will explore five dimensions of discipleship:

- Believe what Jesus believed (transformed mind)
- Live as Jesus lived (transformed character)
- Love as Jesus loved (transformed relationships)
- Minister as Jesus ministered (transformed service)
- Lead as Jesus led (transformed influence)

Christ Existed for Others

Christ was a man for others. He claimed it and he lived it: "The son of man did not come to be served, but to serve, and give his life as a ransom for many" (Matt. 20:28 NKJV). It makes sense, then, that all disciples of Jesus exist for others, and his church exists for others. Just as faith is real only when there is obedience, the church is real only when its faith leads it to become a community for others.

This book is about choosing the life that transforms. It is about what we must do to position ourselves to change. It is subversive by nature because it requires a rethinking of the gospel and how we live it.

Enjoy the exploration.

I

HOW I GOT
TO THIS POINT

If you want to bring fundamental change to people's lives and behavior, a change that will persist and influence others, you need to create a community around them where those new beliefs could be practiced, expressed, and nurtured.[1]

—Malcolm Gladwell,
summarizing the beliefs of John Wesley

I t was a proud moment. We had just commissioned eighty-three new members. The newly initiated made their way off the platform while I descended the steps to get closer to the congregation to begin my sermon. "This is great, isn't it?"

1. Malcolm Gladwell, *The Tipping Point: How Little Things Can Make a Big Difference* (Boston: Little, Brown & Co., 2002), 173.

I began. "But before we get too giddy about new members, let me ask you a question. Why should we bring eighty-three new people into something that is not working?"

That was the first time in thirty years of ministry that I had unmasked myself. I was convinced that the ministry I was leading wasn't working. It appeared to be working, but it just wasn't. "Something is wrong," I said, "and it has been tormenting me for several years. All the formulas, strategic planning, mission statements, and visionary sermons are not making disciples." I had learned one of the preacher's hardest lessons: when your preaching clashes with your environment, environment wins every time.

Where was the personal transformation after all the effort we put into weekend services, Bible studies, small groups, and outreach events? We were engaged in a studied routine of religious activity without change. We were not seeing people come to Christ in any significant number, and people's lives seemed to be the same. We were stuck in the same rut in which so many churches find themselves—religious activity without transformation. We were doing things right, but there was little movement from the Spirit.

I felt like an ice-skater gliding over a frozen lake; just beneath the surface I could see transformation, but I couldn't get at it. That ice represents church infrastructure, customs, and traditions. It represents an institutional community based on roles and hierarchy rather than a community rooted in relationships of trust. It represents pastoral models that insist pastors should be CEOs or experts in church growth instead of shepherds who help people grow in Christ. And yes, often these two roles are mutually exclusive!

As I stood before my congregation that morning, I was prepared to pour out my soul, my desperation. God had been reshaping me for three years. I had morphed in such a way that I could never go back to the way I used to be. Bill Hull the Disciple-Making Pastor had been broken, and now God was starting to reshape me.

For three years people had been steadily trickling out the door of our church. I wouldn't support or agree with much of what they said or did, but God used them as a gift to me. It was the most painful experience of my pastoral life, and so many times I wanted to run away. But God spoke to me very powerfully one morning as I lay prostrate on my office floor: "Bill, I am going to break you. Don't run." I talked about running; I prayed about running; I asked others about finding a better fit. Any job looked better than staying in ministry—a barista at Starbucks, a sportswriter, an Amway salesman. But I couldn't bring myself to do it. Sometimes the only thing that kept me from running was pride. "What would others think?" I thought to myself.

I lived most days hour by hour in survival mode. I was getting older and older—fifty-four, fifty-five, fifty-six. I started getting senior discounts, and I turned my head from retirement commercials. Each day I was less relevant. Each day fewer people cared about me and what I did.

During this "dark night of the soul," I poured my life into three younger men, and one by one they left the church. A plague had descended on the church, and most plagues must run their course. Leaving churches is contagious just as going to churches is contagious. People don't research the facts and then act in accordance with biblical truth. Most often they are swept away by their feelings and by the opinion of friends.

People said I was aloof and unwelcoming. They got the feeling I was on a mission and they were pawns in my plan. They were Bill Hull's projects. But I was doing what I had been taught to do by what I had read about leadership in the twenty-first century. I really thought there was no way I could stay, and there was no place to go. I was in some serious pain.

Then the plague began to lift, attitudes began to change, and it all became very sweet. What happened primarily happened to me, and then it spread. When I humbled myself that Sunday and expressed my frustration and pain, when I admitted that something was wrong and that I was as tired of it as everyone else, we all sighed a gargantuan sigh of relief. The masks came off and we were on our way.

When I finished telling the congregation what God had shown me, they rose up and said *yes* in a way that I have never experienced before in thirty years of ministry. They knew they were no longer my project. They understood deep within that what I was telling them was true. They sensed that something prophetic was happening, and it changed our church.

What I told them was that the Great Commission was more about depth than strategy or technique. I told them discipleship was not optional; being spiritually transformed is the primary and exclusive work of the church. I told them the evidence of being a follower of Jesus is following Jesus. I told them believing the right things was not enough; the faith Jesus taught and lived includes behavioral evidence. I told them the most important question we face is who is saved and who is not. I told them discipleship is a choice; we don't drift into it or amble our way halfheartedly down the path of obedience. I told them I was going to evangelize them. I was going to ask them to *choose the life*—the life of following Jesus, the life that is the answer to the weakness of the church and the boring ineffectiveness of our lives.

WHY I WROTE THIS BOOK

I wrote this book because I couldn't hold it in. More than any other book I have written, God called me to this one. Dietrich Bonhoeffer said, "Christianity without discipleship is always Christianity without Christ."[2] This is a penetrating analysis of both the problem and the solution in many churches today. The problem is that many people believe the right things in their heads about Jesus but do not follow him. The solution is discipleship, which can be summarized as believing what Jesus believed, living the way Jesus lived, loving the way Jesus loved, ministering the way Jesus ministered, and leading the way he led.

2. Dietrich Bonhoeffer, *The Cost of Discipleship* (New York: Macmillan, 1949), 67.

Believing What He Believed (Transformed Mind)

To believe what Jesus believed means we hold a conviction that the life he described in the Sermon on the Mount is possible right now. In fact, Jesus said we can equal and exceed the works that he did (Matt. 5–7; John 14:12–14). This requires a commitment to set aside time to study, pray, and meditate in order to hear the voice of God and to take on the mind of Christ. If that commitment is not present, we are practicing a Christ-less Christianity. After all, how can you follow and learn from someone whose voice you can't recognize?

Living the Way He Lived (Transformed Character)

Too often following Jesus has been limited to admiring the mystery of the God-man and resting in the finished work of the cross. While the basis of a relationship with God in Christ is both his person and his finished work, the ongoing nature of salvation, sometimes called *sanctification,* should not be ignored.

A pathology of the American church has been to disconnect belief from behavior. People think that if you say the right words and believe the right things, you'll receive your get-out-of-hell-free card, and that's it. In the meantime they manage their sin until heaven. Jesus calls us not to sin management but to transformation, where we experience one breakthrough after another and do away with sin in our lives. We are called to follow Jesus and be transformed into his image. We are called to take seriously the character description of Jesus in the Gospels and Philippians 2:5–8. We are expected to take on that same character and thus influence the people around us the same way Jesus influenced others. In short, the gospel connects belief and behavior.

Loving the Way He Loved (Transformed Relationships)

Some of us have settled for loving those who love us and forgiving those who have asked us for forgiveness. We have set limits on how many times we will forgive someone for the same action. The church is marginalized because of estranged relationships and a lack of commitment to follow Jesus. To love as Christ loved is the way to break down the walls that separate us and bring healing to broken lives. Jesus didn't hold anything back and loved until others experienced that love. A community develops character as it pursues the standard summarized by Jesus when he told us to "love each other as I have loved you" (John 15:12).

Ministering the Way He Ministered (Transformed Service)

"The Son of Man did not come to be served, but to serve, and to give his life as a ransom for many" (Matt. 20:28). Jesus ministered out of who he was; his influence came from his character. The way he exercised power was consistent with the humility and submission that governed his character and service (John 14:12–14). As disciples of Jesus we can have the same impact Jesus had.

Leading the Way He Led (Transformed Influence)

Many spiritual leaders find themselves trapped in a church dominated by the surrounding culture of success. Nothing fails like success and that is so true of spiritual leaders who have mimicked models of leadership other than that of Jesus. The leader gets trapped in the "church world's" version of success with its rewards and punishments. The great temptation is to climb the ecclesiastical ladder, but then you find yourself standing on the top of a very short wobbly ladder, and you are sure to fall because there is nothing dependable to hold onto. If the proper markings of success are not present in one's life, consequences follow. Jesus is our leader, and inherent to following him is leading the way he led. Jesus was irrelevant and unnecessary to his culture. And by taking a servant's role, even though it cost him everything, he became the most relevant and necessary man of history.

An Invitation

The solution to the general weakness in the affluent church in the West is spiritual depth, and I define *depth* as living according to the five characteristics of Jesus explained above. This need for depth must begin with the church's leaders. You may recall the story of Jonah and his unwillingness to preach at Nineveh. He booked passage to Tarshish, the ancient Monte Carlo—a place worthy of his skills and calling. The wealthy, cultured pagans needed God just as much as the peasants in Nineveh did, Jonah thought. Jonah was listening not to God's voice but to others that appealed to his prejudice and vanity.

The contemporary spiritual leader also hears many voices. One of the loudest is the one that appeals to the natural desire to be successful. It says you can lead a growing, cutting-edge ministry with all the accoutrements. You can achieve your dreams; you can reach thousands. It tells you to ask God to give you more influence because that is what he desires for you. It is the cultural voice of upward mobility with all its allure. The single greatest need of spiritual leaders today is to ignore this voice of the flesh and learn to hear the voice of God. God is calling us to renounce all other voices and to devote ourselves to hearing his voice. It is an acquired skill—one that I have only begun to learn.

When we see the folly of our ways, we will find, as Jonah did, that throwing overboard the cargo that goes with a trip to Tarshish is not enough; it is time to *jump*. Like Jonah we must jump into the uncertain seas of downward mobility. As Henri Nouwen said, let us be transformed from relevance to prayer, from popularity to ministry, and from leading to being led. I jumped, and as with Jonah, God deposited me right where he wanted me. I invite you to jump with me. You won't be sorry.[3]

3. Henri J. M. Nouwen, *In the Name of Jesus: Reflections on Christian Leadership* (New York: Crossroad, 1989), 25, 49, 71.

2

THE NEED
FOR THE LIFE

Aman came to his pastor and said, "I just want to be a
Christian. I don't want to be a disciple. I like my life
the way it is. I believe that Jesus died for my sins, and I will be
with him when I die. Why do I have to be a disciple?" How
would you answer that question? The answer you give reveals
the gospel you believe and live. Far too often the answer to that
question is "you don't need to be a disciple to go to heaven; it is
not required for eternal life."

The problem we face is a faith that doesn't transform. We
have taught a nondiscipleship Christianity, and in Scripture this
Christianity does not exist. Jesus and Paul both taught that following Jesus is proof of being a Christian (Luke 9:23–25; Phil.
2:1–8).[1] We have made the test for salvation doctrinal rather
than behavioral. We have ritualized salvation with walking the

---

1. There is a tendency to separate the gospel that Jesus taught from the one Paul
developed. Jesus speaks of behavior as the test of a person's faith. This creates a problem

aisle, praying to receive Christ, or signing a doctrinal statement. The trouble with our evangelism is that we have made it so easy to *enter* the Christian life that we miss the repentance, commitment, and regeneration that provide the power to *live* the Christian life.

How often do we meet a person who "accepted Christ" based on a faith that is little more than intellectual assent? A gospel that speaks only of forgiveness of sins and getting into heaven is a partial gospel. The complete gospel says to repent of your sin, take up your cross daily, and follow Jesus.

Yet in the modern church we have lost sight of Jesus as Leader. We relish the fact that he is the sacrificial Lamb and the Savior of the world, but we reject him as our Leader—the one whose life we should imitate. Creedal Christianity has created a church of people who profess the faith but whose lives are disconnected from their words. Jesus as Leader demands a response. When Jesus said, "Follow me . . . and I will make you fishers of men" (Matt. 4:19), James and John dropped their nets and took action. They said *yes* to his invitation. Faith is real only when there is obedience.

The whole point of the gospel is to be transformed into the image of Christ. The apostle Paul wrote to the Christians in Galatia, "My dear children, for whom I am again in the pains of childbirth until Christ is formed in you, how I wish I could be with you now and change my tone, because I am perplexed by you!" (Gal. 4:19–20). Paul's perplexity came not from trying to figure out what the goal was but from trying to help people be shaped into the likeness of Jesus. The English word *formed* in this passage is from the Greek *morphe*, a word familiar to us largely because of computerized videos and graphic design. Romans 12:2 uses the same root word in "be *transformed* by the renewing of your mind" (emphasis added). Another example is found in Romans 8:29: "For those God foreknew he also predestined to be *conformed* to the likeness of his Son" (emphasis added). Trans-

---

for those who feel more comfortable with airtight theology. I find that evangelicals are theologically informed but biblically illiterate in that they adopt theological positions without reading the plain teachings of Scripture.

formation is the goal, but it is not always easy to achieve due to our default settings.

OUR DEFAULT SETTINGS

Computers are programmed with basic settings regarding type size and style, margins, columns, and so on. These are called the *default settings*, so when you create a new document, the same settings come up every time. The church can develop default settings as well. If a church has held to a nondiscipleship Christianity for twenty-five years, a couple of sermons that create temporary inspiration will not change the default settings—the basic belief system.[2] The gospel of salvation as separate from discipleship is the church's default setting, and it is challenging to change it.

In my years as a pastor I have seen a lot of self-inflicted wounding in the church that is deeply troubling. So many choose not to live in the power of the Spirit. In fact, it is highly unusual when Christians return good for evil, bless those who curse them, and pray for those who use them (Luke 6:27–28). The works of the flesh are easier to find than the fruit of the Spirit. Gossip is rampant and so is the tendency to believe the worst of others.

Very few of us share our faith or honor God with 10 percent of our income.[3] Fewer still are devoted to prayer and the spiritual disciplines. Such activities as listening prayer, fasting, solitude, silence, and scriptural meditation are considered practices for only the elite. We have taught that any effort to pursue God is optional and not part of the proof of salvation. Dallas Willard puts it this way: "The 'natural' outcome of all this is what we see among Christians in this country as a visible group. Namely, no real difference in spiritual and moral quality of life from the mass of non-Christians. The life we see among Christians generally is

2. I borrowed this "default" idea from Dallas Willard (sermon notes, small gathering, Denver, 22 September 2002).

3. George Barna, *The State of the Church 2002* (Ventura, Calif.: Barna Research Group, 2002), in Holly Peters, "Evangelicals on the Decline," *Biola Connection*, fall 2002, 10–15.

a result of what they do regularly and are routinely taught. They are the outcome of what those of us who teach and lead intend and expect, or at a very minimum accept!"[4]

The church's default settings must be changed. How much longer can we stomach the reality that our work is fraudulent? How much longer will we allow people to think sin management is acceptable? I raise the white flag of surrender to my sin; I just sin and confess, sin and confess, sin and confess, without expecting victory.

How much longer will we tolerate thinking we cannot really be like Jesus, follow Jesus, and be transformed into his likeness? The problem is that we have given up on everyone being transformed disciples. We have said by our actions that carnal Christianity is acceptable. We have downgraded the norm; it is no longer taking up one's cross daily in an act of self-denial. We have settled for pseudotransformation characterized by external behaviors that pass for holiness. We go after the "hot sins" of adultery and other sexual crimes, but we wink at people who gossip, slander, and hoard. People can be control freaks with selfish ambition and lead lives of worry and fear, and we look the other way. In fact, often these very people are our pastors, elders, and respected members.

BARRIERS TO TRANSFORMATION

In the early 1970s evangelicals burst onto the national scene. They grew in number and might, becoming prominent in presidential elections. Today the secular press pays a great deal of attention to evangelicals, which might indicate they are growing in number and power. The research, however, shows this is not the case. In fact, evangelicals are shrinking in number and losing much of their influence in public life. The number of evangelicals in America has dropped from 17 percent of the total population in 1992 to 12 percent in 2002. While 77 percent of Americans

4. Willard, sermon notes, 22 September 2002.

call themselves Christians, only 12 percent meet the evangelical criteria used by pollster George Barna.[5]

In his critical study *Growing True Disciples*, Barna studied the general Christian populace by scientific means and then interviewed and investigated a number of churches that were engaged in disciple making. Some of his conclusions are that about 52 percent of Christians are making some effort to grow spiritually, but they are inconsistent and get limited results for their efforts. They are more inclined to read a devotional book, participate in a prayer group, or study an outline of their pastor's sermon, with only 17 percent willing to meet weekly with two or three others for accountability.[6] Barna also pointed out barriers to transformation, as follows:

1. They lack passion, perspective, priorities, and perseverance to develop their spiritual lives.
2. Few attend a church that pushes them to grow.
3. Few attend churches that provide resources.
4. Many said that regardless of good intentions, their real passions lie elsewhere.
5. They are too busy; schedule and energy follow greater passions.
6. Most were satisfied to engage in a devotional process without regard to the product in their lives. One sees this most readily in small groups that live on relationship alone and include no missional component.
7. Activities offered are good but not challenging.
8. Not one adult surveyed said his or her goal was to be a committed follower of Jesus. Believers have been trained to test their faith by doctrine rather than behavior. Thus

5. Barna, *State of the Church*. Barna has tightened his definition of an evangelical. His study shows that there are a lot of "non-evangelical born agains" who do not believe the Bible is totally accurate in what it teaches, or that Satan exists, or that Jesus lived a sinless life. The greatest breakdown in difference is that evangelicals believe Jesus is the exclusive means of salvation.

6. George Barna, *Growing True Disciples* (Colorado Springs: Waterbrook, 2001), 49.

the idea of following and doing does not enter into the salvation equation.[7]

In conclusion Barna writes, "Churches have done a good job of promoting the importance of spiritual maturity, but they have mostly failed to provide an environment in which spiritual growth is a lifestyle. Instead of becoming a natural extension of one's spiritual journey, steady spiritual growth has become the exception to the rule, the domain of the spiritual superstars and fanatics."[8] Then Barna makes a dire prediction: "I will argue that unless we embrace a comprehensive and far-reaching commitment to radical change in how we conduct our lives and our ministries, we are doomed to minimal results."[9]

The hard data supports the anecdotal. We have accepted a nondiscipleship gospel that is the source of our demise. We are in decline. We are boring people. It is not working. That is why I poured out my frustration to the congregation. We have a church with good intentions but with a limited commitment to loving God and our neighbors because our leaders are unwilling or cannot agree on what it means to make disciples. Some are afraid to admit they have no experience in teaching transformation.

NONDISCIPLESHIP CHRISTIANITY

Generally people agree the church in the West continues to decline. However, many have not noticed how serious the problem is among evangelicals. The question that must be answered is, What is the nature of salvation? Who is saved and who is not? If millions of professing Christians think they are regenerate because of a doctrinal test alone, this would explain why many Christians don't witness and give a meager 2 percent to God's work. It would explain why many who profess Christianity drive expensive cars;

7. Ibid., 54.
8. Ibid., 55.
9. Ibid.

live in large, elaborate homes; and are financially leveraged to the max. It would explain why missionaries can't raise their support and churches struggle financially. It would explain why there are so many divorces in the church. It would explain the vast accommodation to culture in churches and why our most talented members look elsewhere for investment of their time and energy.

What if 30 to 50 percent of our evangelical congregations are populated and being led by the unsaved? That is a frightening thought, but I suggest that the heart of the weakness is our teaching. We have taught a nondiscipleship Christianity, so why should it be any surprise that over 50 percent of professing Christians have opted out? We have taught faith as agreement, instead of commitment to follow Jesus.

The average group of professing Christians would agree that we all should love and obey God, that the Great Commandment and the Great Commission are our main purposes, and that we should share our faith and give sacrificially of our time and resources. The problem is that while we say these are what should define Christian character, Christians themselves do not exhibit these qualities.

I am reminded of how my children used to respond when I told them to clean up their rooms. They often told me they would do it, but later. Much to my chagrin, hours later their rooms were untouched. They had agreed, but they didn't do it. I am happy to say that at home I had some recourse, ways to punish their failure to keep their promises. In the church, however, what do you do? If we started throwing out everyone who doesn't follow Jesus, not only would it be scandalous, but most churches would close!

The only measure of salvation is whether we choose to live the life to which Jesus called us. According to Jesus, living this life is part and parcel to the gospel. That is why I have concluded that discipleship or spiritual formation is the primary and exclusive work of the church. Everything else we do is, in the words of Solomon, "a chasing after the wind" (Eccles. 2:26).

Many churches have limited disciple making to a postconversion training period, but this is a poor excuse for biblical discipleship. We must remember that discipleship is not one of the things the church does, it is *the* thing the church does!

A disciple is a learner who is to become like his or her teacher, but that's not what we've been teaching.[10] We have taught that discipleship is optional, a temporary experience, and have kept it in the confines of the church. This is why the church has not multiplied in a healthy way throughout the entire world. We keep spreading a weakened, nonreproductive gospel.

BOREDOM

One of the most telling indicators that we have a nondiscipleship Christianity is boredom within the church. There seems to be nothing compelling about our vision of the Christian life. The reason attendance has slipped among evangelicals in recent years is because once you are bar-coded into the family, there is nothing left to do except church work.[11] I know this is hard for some of us to swallow, but church work does not stimulate most people. It makes small what God meant to be big.

We have forgotten that the kingdom of God is about Christ's rule in every facet of life (Col. 1:27). Going to church is a significant but small part of most Christians' lives. When we limit the Christian mission to fixing our churches and making them work better, we have insulted Christ and his call on our lives. I think of the late Richard Halverson, who was a wonderful pastor and for many years the chaplain of the U.S. Senate. When he was pastor of Fourth Presbyterian Church in Washington, D.C., he was asked where his church was located. He answered that it was scattered throughout the entire region. Yes, the meetings were held at a given place once a week, but the church's real function occurred in the many places of government, home, school, and business in the area.

10. When a disciple is fully taught, he will be like his teacher (Luke 6:40).
11. The number of evangelicals in the United States has dropped from 17 percent of the population in 1992 to 12 percent in 2002. Barna, *State of the Church*.

The degree to which the kingdom of God is revealed in these many places depends on the individual's commitment to live the life that Jesus lived. The Great Commission has more to do with depth than strategy. The awful truth is that we are making very little impact on culture because we are shallow. And we are shallow because we have separated salvation from discipleship.

When I started teaching that to choose Christ means to choose following him and experiencing transformation, members of our church came alive. They saw something wonderful they had missed. God could change their ideas and their feelings; they could become different people who *wanted* to do the things Jesus did. For many, the boredom that once characterized their lives went away.

FIRST-CENTURY DISCIPLESHIP

The starting point for turning things around is a fuller understanding of what the disciples heard Jesus say when he told them to "make disciples." The first thing Peter, Matthew, James, and company must have thought when Jesus said this is that they should go find and develop other people like themselves. It is clear this is what Paul had in mind many years later (2 Tim. 2:2).[12] To Christ's disciples, *discipleship* meant making a serious commitment to follow a leader.

In the first century a young man could join one of a variety of different rabbinical schools. Each school was led by a rabbi or teacher. Evidence from history suggests that in some cases students chose their teacher, and teachers had the privilege of accepting or rejecting their applications. The competition may have been similar to that in nations whose students must pass exams that determine the direction of their careers. Disciples of first-century Judaism learned everything from their teacher. They learned his stories and his life habits. They learned to keep the Sabbath his way as well as his interpretations of the Torah. When a disciple learned everything

12. The command to teach others who could teach others is a convincing proof that Jesus, Peter, and then Paul all were on the same page as to how to spread the gospel.

his teacher knew, he would go and teach his own disciples. If by Bar Mitzvah a young man hadn't achieved what was expected of him, he would be rejected and then would return to a life of one of the professions—farming, fishing, carpentry, and the like. This is one of the reasons Jesus and his followers were looked down upon by the religious establishment. They were men of the professions.

From this model of first-century discipleship, we can infer some principles for discipleship today. While it is clear that discipleship was practiced in a more informal way as well, when the Twelve heard "make disciples of all nations" (Matt. 28:19), they would have thought of submissive followers and learners like themselves. The idea of discipleship without submission to a leader was unthinkable back then.

Discipleship today must also begin with a commitment of *submission to at least one other person.* Choosing the life begins right here. *Without this relational dimension, everything that follows is weakened.*

The teacher-disciple relationship was a powerful bond in the first century. It was as important as and in many cases more crucial than a father-son relationship. It was similar to a servant-master relationship (Matt. 10:24). Once accepted as a disciple, a young man would work his way up the discipleship ladder. He would begin as a *talmidh*, or beginner, who would be required to sit in the back of the room and not speak. Later he became a distinguished student who could begin taking an independent line in his approach or questioning. The next level was a disciple-associate; at this stage he could sit immediately behind the rabbi during prayer time. The highest level was when the disciple reached "disciple of the wise" status, when he was recognized as the intellectual equal of his rabbi.[13]

Oral tradition was the primary mode of study. Disciples learned the teacher's words verbatim so they could pass them along to the next generation. They often had to learn up to four interpretations of each major passage in the Torah.

13. Michael Wilkens, *The Concept of Disciple in Matthew's Gospel* (New York: E. J. Brill, 1988), 123.

Disciples also needed to know how their teacher kept the commands of God—how he practiced the Sabbath, fasted, prayed, and said blessings in ceremonial situations. They also learned the rabbi's teaching methods and all the traditions, which were many.

Jesus said, "A disciple . . . [who] is fully taught will be like his teacher" (Luke 6:40 RSV). The highest calling of any disciple was to imitate his teacher. Paul called upon Timothy to follow his example (2 Tim. 3:10–14), and he didn't hesitate to call upon all believers to do the same (1 Cor. 4:14–16; 11:1; Phil. 4:9; 2 Tim. 2:2). The problem today is that while a pastor may be a good example with regard to character, the pastor usually is not close enough to members of his or her congregation to influence them personally. The pastor's life is distant, insulated from the marketplace and the public square; thus he or she isn't a mentor to the ordinary person.

Finally, in the first century there was a clear, nonnegotiable expectation that every disciple would reproduce in finding and training his own apprentices. He was to start his own school, and he could call it after his name. It was common for a disciple's school to be called the "House of Hillel" or the "House of Joshua."

A CLEAR DISTINCTION

The characteristics above describe the institution of discipleship as it was practiced in the first century.[14] Jesus implemented this same institution with his closest followers, and they were expected to reproduce. When he called upon them to make disciples, they were to find others who would make the commitments above. When he told them to "[teach] them to obey everything I have commanded you" (Matt. 28:20), they knew it would require the kind of dedication outlined above.

There was a crucial difference, however, in Jesus' teaching, which is shown in his strong reaction to the Pharisees' hypocrisy. He scolded them for their selfish ambition and propensity for showmanship.

---

14. Four of the five observations are a product of the website http://www.Rabbi Yeshua.com by Kehilat Sar Shalom.

They love to be greeted in the marketplaces and to have men call them "Rabbi." But you are not to be called "Rabbi," for you have only one Master and you are all brothers. And do not call anyone on earth "father," for you have one Father, and he is in heaven. Nor are you to be called "teacher," for you have one Teacher, the Christ. The greatest among you will be your servant. For whoever exalts himself will be humbled, and whoever humbles himself will be exalted.

Matthew 23:7–12

The New Testament does refer to people as teachers, elders, and so on, but that was not Jesus' meaning in this passage. He was speaking against being a slave or servant to any master other than himself. As a disciple in the first century, you followed your master and did whatever he told you to do. If you ever asked your rabbi a question, you were bound by his answer. That is why people were cautious about asking their teacher questions.

The distinction that Jesus made was that his disciples were not to raise up new disciples for themselves. They were not to start their own school or academy. The disciples of Jesus were never to take the role of master. In fact, Jesus' disciples were forbidden to make their own disciples. They were to raise up more disciples for Jesus, and the same is true today. Yes, we will have teachers, mentors, and leaders, but they never will become our masters. The job of Jesus' disciples today is the same as it was in the first century. We are called to follow Jesus and to raise up more disciples for him.[15]

FIRST THINGS FIRST

Before we can make disciples, however, we must be disciples. Before a congregation or any group can choose the life, pastors and leaders must choose the life. It is not automatic. It doesn't

15. I want to thank Pastor Thomas Lancaster of Kehilat Sar Shalom for his helpful insights that provided guidance for me in this section.

come with a seminary degree or a set of ministry skills. It is a commitment to be transformed; it is a choice we make, an intention to live the way Jesus lived.

The deepest sin of my life is holding onto the right to lead my own life. I am a high achiever. I like to be in control. I enjoy accomplishment. I love to "go for it." I like to think that I have all kinds of options available to me, that I can create, create, create. If I want to be transformed, I have to give that all up. I must confess my sin of insisting on leading my own life.

That is how I got started. I humbled myself and asked God to lead me. I know it sounds trite and common, but when you get it, when you understand what it means to choose the life of following Jesus, it is the most liberating experience in life. Jesus said it for us: "No one can serve two masters. Either he will hate the one and love the other, or he will be devoted to the one and despise the other" (Matt. 6:24). We must choose.

DISCIPLESHIP TODAY

The etymological definition of *disciple* is "learner."[16] The cultural understanding as experienced in the first century was that of "follower." Other valid definitions focus on character and behavior.[17] All who commit their lives to Christ are his disciples.[18] One can possess all these credentials and yet miss the key part of being a follower of Jesus, and that is *following someone who can teach you how to follow Jesus*. A disciple is someone who is in submission to

16. *Manthano* means to learn or find out; understand; hear. F. Wilbur Gingrich, *Shorter Lexicon of the Greek New Testament* (Chicago: University of Chicago Press, 1965), 131.

17. In an earlier book I have defined a disciple as having characteristics from John 15:7–13. (1) A disciple remains in Christ through the Word and prayer. (2) A disciple bears much fruit. (3) A disciple responds in obedience. (4) A disciple is contented. (5) A disciple loves as Christ loved. Bill Hull, *Disciple-Making Pastor* (Grand Rapids: Revell, 1988), chap. 3.

18. My position is that all who believe in Christ are identified as disciples at the moment of spiritual birth. Matthew 28:19 says that the first part of making a disciple is evangelism, which is why disciples should be baptized. But we will continue to clarify what it means to truly believe.

at least one other person in a healthy and appropriate relation-ship in which the disciple has the support and accountability to develop fully as a follower of Jesus. The church is packed with people who claim to be followers of Jesus, but they are not con-nected in community; they are going solo. To them discipleship is what a person does in a program. Their thinking is, "I engage in only the activities or spiritual exercises I have time for or what seems attractive to me. In other words, I maintain control of Jesus' agenda for me. I keep my distance from anyone who might threaten my autonomy."

To be a disciple as described by Jesus requires a person to submit himself or herself to a more mature follower of Jesus. Unless you have done so, you are not following Jesus in the way he desired. Our definition of a disciple, then, must be adjusted to fit what Jesus truly meant. We know this is what he meant by the way he lived and by what he modeled in calling the Twelve to be with him. We also see this in the way he changed his rela-tionship to them when he was ready to commission them to go make their own disciples (Mark 3:14–16).[19]

The purpose of discipleship is to go deeper with God, to be shaped into the image of Christ, because character is developed in community. If we are following the New Testament model, discipleship should look like this today:

1. A disciple submits to a teacher who teaches him or her how to follow Jesus.
2. A disciple learns Jesus' words.
3. A disciple learns Jesus' way of ministry.
4. A disciple imitates Jesus' life and character.
5. A disciple finds and teaches other disciples for Jesus.

19. Jesus called the Twelve to be with him so they could eventually go out to preach. He graduated them in the upper room when he said, "I no longer call you servants, be-cause a servant does not know his master's business. Instead, I have called you friends, for everything that I learned from my Father I have made known to you" (John 15:15). This demonstrates that they are now moving from being disciples to the responsibility of making their own disciples.

How common is this kind of discipleship in the church? I can count on one hand the churches I know that incorporate all five of the discipleship principles I just laid out. It is quite common to find ministries with three of the five, a small minority with four of the five, but almost none of them (including my church) practice all five. The most common characteristics are:

2. A disciple learns Jesus' words.
3. A disciple learns Jesus' way of ministry.
4. A disciple imitates Jesus' life and character.

The reason characteristics 2 through 4 are most common is that they are the least challenging of the five. Frankly, people can do these without having to change. It goes back to the indictment that we have found ways to be Christian without becoming Christlike. Items 1 and 5 make it all work. I don't mean 2 through 4 are unimportant; indeed, they are vital. But learning about Jesus' words, ministry, and character does not require you to submit yourself to the authority of Christ through another person, nor does it require you to find and develop your own disciples.

The frightening truth is that most Christians fail to even do 2 through 4, let alone 1 and 5. But what scares me more is that we can practice 2 through 4 alone and be considered mature Christian leaders. The fact that we avoid submission and seldom evangelize and disciple is a troublesome fact of the body of Christ.

When I called my fellow Christians to choose the life, I told them that it included submitting to at least one other person. I told them the days of arm's-length, nondiscipleship Christianity were over. The rest of the staff and I called on them to make that commitment, and over one hundred of them did. It was a starting point—a place to stand and to begin. We started our own Choose the Life Society, composed of those who made a public declaration to take up their cross and follow Jesus. We in no way stood in judgment of those who didn't join the society, but the society provided a fresh opportunity for those who were weary of religious activity without change.

Churches ought to be outposts of the kingdom—sending centers for the real work that is done in the various sectors of life. This is how one life affects another life where we live, work, and play (see 2 Tim. 2:2). The personal connection of a teacher ensures transformation because character is developed in community, and the expectation of finding and training your own disciples ensures multiplication. Without characteristics 1 and 5 the closed system will continue and so will our inability to reach others.

A Disciple Submits to a Teacher

The primary reason most people don't grow is they never get to the number one dimension of discipleship. There is nothing more fundamental to spiritual maturity. Character is developed in community, and that development begins only with submission. Paul taught that submission was for everyone; it was evidence of being filled with the Spirit (Eph. 5:21). It was the basic trait that made Jesus attractive to us (Phil. 2:5–8). God is opposed to the proud and gives grace to the humble. God asks for and rewards our humility. This is one of the easiest commands to dodge. I mean, who isn't humble before God? But what the New Testament really teaches is that humility is revealed in our relationship to other believers. *Submission is proof of humility*, and that is why character is built in community. It requires checking my autonomy in at the door. The other person helps me keep my commitments to God.

The genius of submission is that it is a two-way street. Since no one is master, both are servants of Jesus, both benefit greatly from the relationship. One person is generally the more seasoned and could be considered the lead teacher who is showing the other person what it means to follow Jesus. This provides the strength required to hold people together as they face the challenges to faith. Many people who don't have this kind of support go into destructive tailspins. They usually emerge later, but much time is lost. Even more well-intentioned believers drift and find themselves nearly comatose spiritually, numbed by years of religious activity without transformation.

The attachment to another like-minded person in mutual submission and humility brings everything out of hiding and into the light. It rescues the process of learning Jesus' words, ways, and life from individualism. When we are protected within the walls of our personal autonomy, we can nestle down and avoid character development.

Once we have been discipled and had our own lives transformed, we are ready to move to characteristic 5. This is the other truly radical dimension of making disciples as they did in the first century. This dimension brings it all to life; it is what gives the disciple-making process a pulse.

A Disciple Finds and Teaches Other Disciples

The reason disciple making and its subtext called discipleship is a failure in most churches is because of the lack of an expectation that it will reproduce other disciples. As I look out at my congregation week after week, what do I see? I see people sitting in the same places, talking to the same people at about the same time before and after services. Our services are about the same each week—songs, sermon, testimony, offering, etc.—and all of us know an awful lot about Jesus. We have spent much of our lives meeting with other believers in what we would call a discipleship relationship. We have learned Jesus' words; we have learned his ways of doing ministry; we have dedicated ourselves to imitate his character. And there we sit very much the same this year as last, near the same empty seats in about the same places. We try to witness whenever we can, when the opportunity arises, but let's face it, we barely have a pulse.

Yet we wonder why our church isn't doing better, why we don't have outreaches that fill our church and make us the place to be. The reason is that we believe making disciples is optional and have reduced spiritual development to an in-house, nonthreatening experience. When we do only the first four of the five dimensions of disciple making taught by Jesus, we just meet with ourselves. We talk to ourselves. We interact about ourselves. We address the issues that are about us. We are trapped in a closed system. And holding six evangelistic events a year is not the cure.

Once we are "fully taught," the expectation is that we will find and teach other disciples for Jesus. That is what the Great Commission is about: I have trained you, now you go do the same thing.[20] We have not followed Jesus in this way. Most of us know it, and I am willing to admit it. How would making disciples look on the ground in the flow of twenty-first-century life?

The Choose the Life Society at my former church had over one hundred members. We were all meeting in groups of two or three over the course of a year. We followed a curriculum that contained a variety of flexible and need-based resources. The goal the first year was to break through growth barriers and go deeper with God, to gain significant momentum in morphing into the image of Christ. But what came next? The answer was to reproduce. That meant these one hundred people each would have to choose a new person to meet with for the next year. Instead of one hundred plus people meeting, there would be two hundred or more. *But if those new one hundred come from our own church, we still would have a closed system.* The new disciples should not be people who are already in the church; they should come from the harvest field. There are a number of methods that need to be used to evangelize. There is a place for the media, campaigns, crusades, and the like. But the basic model that penetrates culture best is the model that begins with our own relational networks.

I suspect it is true that we are more committed to packing our churches than penetrating our culture. But penetrating our culture is the heart of making disciples. What will we do?

CHOOSE THE LIFE AND WALKING TOGETHER

Making disciples begins with an evangelism that is different than the evangelism with which most of us are familiar. This new kind of

20. Jesus was very consistent on this. See Matthew 28:18–20; John 15:15–16; Acts 1:8.

evangelism requires prayer and the building of a relationship with a person. Rather than treating evangelism like a business transaction, we should treat it like the process of making a disciple.

I asked Alan Andrews, U.S. Director of the Navigators, "If you started from scratch with an interested unbeliever, what would you do?" His response provided the following practical outline:

1. *Let's Walk Together.* Evangelism should begin with friendship, which is usually built around common interests; you just happen to click with a person. "Let's walk together on this journey" is the spirit of this first step.
2. *Introduce Them to Community.* Since all character is built in community, take them to your community. This could be a small group of friends or the community of your church.
3. *Teach Them the Spiritual Disciplines.* This is 2 through 4 of the five characteristics of first-century discipleship. By observing your example, the new disciple begins to learn Jesus' words, learn Jesus' ways of ministry, and imitate Jesus' life and character.
4. *Teach Them How to Live among Unbelievers.* The new Christian can now imitate how you lived next to him or her when he or she was an unbeliever.

This fourth step assumes that eventually the person committed his or her life to Christ and has learned how to follow Jesus by following you. It is incumbent upon you, the spiritual leader, to teach by example. This means that pastors and church leaders must teach their disciples how to live among unbelievers, which may require a radical change in how time is spent and with whom if this is not already being modeled by the leadership.

This strikes at the root of the church problem. The institution of the church too often gobbles up time and energy on sin management, blocking leaders from living powerfully among unbelievers. This goes back to the strength of commitment to penetrate the world around us. But this new ground is taken one person at a time.

THE GREATEST OMISSION
IN THE GREAT COMMISSION

We have created many omissions in the Great Commission. Jesus said,

> All authority in heaven and on earth has been given to me. Therefore *go* and make disciples of *all* nations, baptizing them in the name of the Father and of the Son and of the Holy Spirit, and *teaching* them to obey everything I have commanded you. And surely I am with you always, to the very end of the age.
>
> Matthew 28:18–20, emphasis added

But we have made "go" optional. We have changed "all" to "some." We have changed "teaching them to obey" to "suggesting that they obey." The greatest and most debilitating omission, however, is that we have made disciple making an insular process in a closed system. We have not taught our disciples to live among unbelievers because we don't know how to do it ourselves. We walked into a church and have never really left or gone to the world. Oh, we do go to work and interact with the world as citizens, parents, workers, and so on, but we have not gone to the world en masse as disciple makers.

What I'm proposing is a radical departure from the norm. Most good and godly church members will look at you with befuddlement when this concept is presented. It is so different from what we have been taught and requires a very different focus and effort.

We must choose the life—the life of discipleship as practiced and taught by Jesus and lived out by his first-century followers. We must courageously cast aside our nondiscipleship Christianity and submit ourselves to a life of accountability, personal transformation, and making disciples among the unbelieving. This is our primary and exclusive work. This is faith as Jesus taught it. To do anything less is failure.

3

THE CALL TO THE LIFE

Christianity has no cost in America. We've made it
way too easy to be "born again"—perhaps much easier than Jesus intended. When do we get to the point
at which we accept smaller numbers of intensely devoted people rather than feverishly investing in filling
auditoriums and stadiums with massive numbers of
the lukewarm "Christians" that Jesus promised to
spew from his mouth?[1]

—George Barna

I have drunk the same cocktail of frustration regarding
the church as George Barna. I know what it feels like to
look out at a congregation and wonder if I should bless them

1. George Barna, "Barna's Beefs #5," in *The State of the Church 2002* (Ventura, Calif.:
Barna Research Group, 2002), in Holly Peters, "Evangelicals on the Decline," *Biola Connection*, fall 2002, 10–15.

or ask God to open the ground and swallow us all. We have separated discipleship from spiritual formation—a mammoth error in our hermeneutic that has led to disaster. It has made discipleship seem programmed and superficial. It has partitioned off spiritual formation from the common believer and until recently imprisoned it in the academy.[2] But I know if we had smaller numbers of intensely devoted followers of Jesus, as Barna suggests, we wouldn't stay small very long. We must have a passion to multiply, to live among unbelievers and make disciples where we live.

It is time for the church at large to do the right thing, to return our ministries to the kind of disciple making that was taught by Jesus and practiced by his disciples. It is time to commit to going deep with God, believing that the depth of personal transformation is the mother lode in fulfilling the Great Commission. The first act of a disciple is obedience, not a confession.

It is worth noting that many have stopped using classic disciple-making language. Because of some disillusionment with discipleship, the biblical language died and a new language was needed. *Spiritual formation* has become the new term for discipleship. I would encourage the restoration of traditional language because the new language allows adherents to separate spiritual formation from following Jesus. The Christian experience at its heart is trusting in Jesus enough to follow him, and that is discipleship. I am concerned that spiritual formation will be hijacked by unbelievers and that there will be a tendency to separate the development of the inner life from obedience, from discipleship, and from the Great Commission.

Something must be done, and I am happy to say that something is being done to restore transformational discipleship to

2. By *academy* I mean seminaries and monasteries. Until just a few years ago evangelicals wouldn't touch the spiritual formation movement because of its liberal and Catholic roots. I am thrilled that now, thanks to Eugene Peterson, Dallas Willard, James Houston, and many others, the call to lifelong spiritual transformation is being restored to the church. It is also vital that the discipleship movement and the spiritual formation movement merge into a balanced tour de force to advance the kingdom.

the church. The classic discipleship that has been practiced in the past fifty years has done much good. But it falls short in that it has been too programmed, too superficial, and frankly too passé for many leaders. Fill-in-the-blank Bible studies and check-off lists of tasks have ceased to appeal to new generations. There is a resistance to Jesus' call to discipleship among his followers. Among general believers this resistance can be traced to the teaching that discipleship is optional. For the pastor or leader it can be traced to the truncated version of discipleship taught in seminaries that goes no further than establishing new believers. The cost to the kingdom of this dismissal is incalculable and inexcusable but, I am glad to say, not unforgivable or unchangeable.

THE CALL TO FOLLOW

It is inappropriate for anyone other than Jesus to issue the call to choose the life. His clear and unequivocal words reach over the centuries to describe what he wants from us. They penetrate our minds and hearts and have a cleansing effect. However, the church's cardiovascular system is clogged with immature disciples who agree with all we've said but who have said *no* to the life. Spiritual greatness in our culture is measured by size—size of churches, size of book sales, size of crowds at special events. The two best-selling books in the world last year were *The Prayer of Jabez* and *Left Behind.* But in the same year church attendance stagnated, the evangelical population decreased, and only half of evangelicals believed it is their responsibility to tell others about Christ.[3] It's time for intervention, to challenge our addiction to mediocrity, and to do the right thing. Jesus called upon us to live differently, to step out of the status quo and step into the life he planned for us in eternity past and provided for us via the cross.

3. Barna, *State of the Church,* 83.

Then he said to them all: "If anyone would come after me, he must deny himself and take up his cross daily and follow me. For whoever wants to save his life will lose it, but whoever loses his life for me will save it. What good is it for a man to gain the whole world, and yet lose or forfeit his very self?"

Luke 9:23–25

Faith is not just believing in your head that Jesus is the Christ; we must prove our faith by following him. Jesus is our Leader, but we don't act like it. We have treated him as Savior of the world, the Lamb that was slain, our resurrected Lord, and our soon-coming King, and there isn't a thing wrong with that. It is a vast oversight, however, that we have not treated him as our Leader. And because of this, transformation has no *traction*. Quite often it seems as though we have forgotten his way of teaching, training, and doing works of power. We have neutered his personality, taken all the spice, humor, intolerance, and straightforwardness from him.

OTHER THINGS DISCIPLES FOLLOW

We are told to follow our gifting, and sometimes we are exhorted to follow our Myers-Briggs personality profile. How many times have we been told to follow our hearts or our dreams? I know that most people who advocate such routes don't mean to recommend not following Jesus. But consider this: My gifting is to serve others and build up the church (1 Peter 4:10–11). A few years ago I considered taking a new position. I was being interviewed by a trusted friend. He confronted me with this very issue, saying, "Bill, do you want to serve in this role, or are you just looking for a place to exercise your gifts?" I had to confess that I was thinking gifts. I was taught to understand God's leading in conjunction with the opportunity to use my skills.

As for following dreams, they too can be tainted. I am sure my dreams for ministry, for example, are soiled with my selfishness and need to be noticed and adored. There is a reason we should not follow our hearts; they are unreliable and even deceitful (Jer. 17:9). There are so many tempting and right-sounding rivals to following Jesus.

ANYONE CAN AND SHOULD DO IT

To choose the life is to choose a way of life. It is a life of self-denial and submission to others. We don't just amble our way into it; it is a conscious decision to live by faith. To choose the life is to join others who have committed to follow Jesus. It is fundamentally about giving up the right to run your own life. You can follow your heart, your dreams, your gifts, and your personality profile, and you can seek the right fit, but all that is inferior to following Jesus.

The first calling of any pastor is to engage in discipleship evangelism in church. I unashamedly confessed to my former congregation that I was engaging in evangelizing them to choose a life of discipleship, to forsake nondiscipleship Christianity with its passive-aggressive individualism, which is really a smoke screen for preserving one's autonomy. Nondiscipleship Christianity stunts growth and robs people of joy and personal accomplishment. People who adhere to it lock themselves out from God's plan and dream for their lives.

There is good evidence that Jesus was speaking only to his closest followers when he issued the call to the life. Some conclude on this basis that Christ's call was just for a select few. This view has done so much damage. It is hard to believe that thinking people would adhere to such an idea, but it has stuck to the church like superglue. Leaders are often the culprits here; we have made it acceptable to be Christian without becoming Christlike. We have taught that a serious, devout life is optional, that it is not the evidence of salvation. It grieves me that in practice I myself have been party to such deception. Far too often we teach high commitment as the norm, but then in practice

47

we accept casual Christianity as normal and see discipleship as fit only for a select few.

Even if Jesus were only speaking to a select few at the time, his use of "anyone" in Luke 9:23 clarifies that he intended his words to apply to all of us. One of the great lies in the church is this: Spiritual greatness is for the few. The kind of commitment to which Jesus called us is really for the super saints—those we write books about, those on whom we bestow honorary degrees. It is to be expected that most of us will simply react to life and hang on. We will struggle along, but we probably won't go full throttle after Jesus.

I have a novel idea. Instead of listening to the pollsters and pundits, why don't we let Jesus tell us who he is and isn't calling? Following Jesus is what a disciple does. It is the norm, and anything else is odd and in need of repair. Following Jesus is for the person who hasn't read a book in thirty years, the woman with four children under foot, the seasoned saint who has all the information but needs stimulation, the teenage boy who just committed his life to Christ. It doesn't matter if you are young or old, healthy or sick—we are all called to follow him. Jesus has issued the call. Will we answer? Why would we choose anything else?

DISCIPLESHIP AND SPIRITUAL FORMATION AS ELITIST

Advocates of going deeper are predominantly religious professionals: monks, ministers, missionaries, theologians, and religious writers. These theologically trained people tend to see choosing the life as reading ancient books, studying the desert fathers, and meditating long hours on the Scripture. Those who are well-read and highly educated can experience spiritual transformation through reading *The Confessions of Saint Augustine*, *The Imitation of Christ*, by Thomas à Kempis, *The Interior Castle*, by Teresa of Avila, or more contemporary works by Henri Nouwen or Thomas Merton.

If these spiritual formation advocates were to attempt to spread the movement in the way it has blessed them, it will almost certainly fail. Most people are not contemplative; most are not drawn to the monastic life. So we must go beyond educational levels, beyond temperaments, beyond learning styles. When Jesus said "anyone" that is what he meant, so part of our quest is to find ways to practice spiritual disciplines in different ways and levels. The life of spiritual transformation is also for the uneducated, the nonreader, the action-oriented, and those who are repulsed by structure. (See chapter 4 for a further discussion.)

SELF-DENIAL IS ESSENTIAL

Four words that make the strong tremble: "He must deny himself" (Mark 8:34). Everyone admires self-denial in others but dislikes the idea of practicing it themselves. The reason for this is that we have misunderstood what Jesus was asking for. C. S. Lewis gave me the most important insight on this passage. He believed that self-denial in and of itself is no virtue, that denying oneself life's pleasures just to say you did so is the apex of arrogance. Self-denial as a virtue is rooted in the ascetic world of hair shirts and simulated crucifixions. Father Anthony, the founder of Christian monasticism, never changed his vest or washed his feet. Simeon Stylites spent the last thirty-six years of his life atop a fifty-foot pillar. The ascetic lives a life of rigorous self-denial. The spirit is good and the body is bad, so never get into a Jacuzzi or get a massage, and never do anything that would tempt you to say, "Boy, does that feel good."

I love the words of nineteenth-century Scottish preacher Alexander MacLaren, "Any asceticism is a great deal more to men's taste than abandoning self. They would rather stick hooks in their backs and do the swinging poojah than give up their sins and yield up their wills."[4] I recall a passage from *The Spiritual Ex-*

4. Alexander MacLaren, quoted on www.Preachingtoday.com. *Poojah* comes from the Swing Festival of the Hindus. The performer is suspended from a mast by hooks passed

ercises of St. Ignatius in which he recommended opening a window in foul weather in order to identify with the sufferings of Jesus. I'm with C. S. Lewis on this; there is no need to suffer without purpose. What Jesus was asking for was very specific.

Say No to Self in order to Say Yes to God

Self-denial's only righteous role is to eliminate any obstacle that blocks our saying *yes* to God. As both MacLaren and Lewis mention, *Jesus is asking me to deny myself the right to be in charge of my own life.* It is self-denial that makes it possible for me to submit my will to his will. He wants to lead and asks me to follow. That drives a stake through the heart of my will, my ego, my desire to control.

If we are Jesus' servants, we deny ourselves the right to justice in human relationships; we deny ourselves the right to a good reputation and vindication while on earth. That is what Jesus' life was like—he gave up his rights to be worshiped as God and instead was rejected, slandered, and killed. Jesus asks us to deny ourselves reliance on that ten-year plan that we worked out with a battery of psychological tests and a financial planner. He asks us to deny ourselves control over others' opinions of us. He asks us to deny ourselves success as the world defines it, as the church defines it, and as we define it.

A young man was writing a paper on pastoral ministry and came to interview me. He began with a question I had never been asked before. "What has been your greatest sacrifice as a pastor?" I sat there for a moment relishing the opportunity to explore my mind for the answer. Then it came to me very clearly, "I think it is the discipline to treat certain people better than they deserve to be treated." Some people deserve to be told off, rebuked, and straightened out, but as a pastor I must always be careful how I treat them and hold my tongue. I let them shoot

through the muscle over the shoulder blade and then whirled round so as to fly out centrifugally. I assume it would hurt terribly and somehow made them feel more virtuous.

at me, accuse me, and blame me for their problems. I let them hold me to a higher standard than they have for themselves. Of course this isn't always pleasant, but treating people better than they deserve is the gospel. It is the kingdom of God, the heart of Jesus, and the essence of love. What I have denied myself is the freedom to speak my mind and let people have it. But that is still not my greatest act of self-denial.

The Greatest Self-Denial

The greatest sacrifice I have had to make is to give up the right to control my own future, to direct the way my life should go. I had to decide that Jesus would lead and I would follow. I have always been a high achiever and an aggressive, go-for-it type guy. I had spent my life creating and taking advantage of opportunities. My natural bent was to follow my vision, dreams, and heart and then periodically check behind me to make sure Jesus was blessing it. It is a titanic struggle daily for me to allow Jesus to lead.

I live parallel lives—one as a writer and a second as a spokesman for the disciple-making movement. My mind is alive with concepts and ideas of how to advance the agenda. It isn't unusual for me to become so excited about an idea that I jump up and down, clap my hands, and hoot and holler.

When I was leading, I would be headlong into the project, making phone calls and writing e-mails. But now that Jesus is leading and I'm following, I pray and ask God to provide the confirmation through others in the body and by providing the resources in people and funds. Most importantly, I now force myself to deeply question my motives and what is really going on inside of me.

I have a friend who says he is committed not to make anything happen on his own. At first I questioned his commitment as far too passive, but I have come to agree with his position. What he meant is to give God time to prepare the way, to provide prepared hearts and the resources for the challenge ahead. In denying myself the right to run my own life, I give up control of the timing and the method of my actions and submit my dreams, visions, and breakthrough ideas to God's leadership. I will deny myself in order to say *yes* to God.

TAKE UP YOUR MISSION

The cross was central to Jesus' mission and it is a metaphor for ours. Those who have chosen the life, who have denied themselves the right to run their own lives, will find their cross waiting for them on the path of obedience. That is when we pick it up.

Yet many of us live our lives with the perpetual question, "Lord, what do you want me to do; what is my mission?" The common mistake is that we seek the answer to this question before we start walking the path of obedience. This is exemplified by nearly 50 percent of churchgoers who attend services a couple of times a month, throw something in the offering that is below 2 percent of their income, and hope to hear something that will get them through the week. They don't see themselves as disciples, learners, or followers of Jesus. They believe self-denial is for monks, missionaries, and ministers. They go through life being Christian without being Christlike. They never pick up their cross because they never submit themselves to true discipleship. In fairness to them, sad to say, often no one has taught them what following Jesus really means.

The Way It Works

First we choose the life; we join the Society of Jesus. That means we set aside any competing priorities and follow him. Then our mission is revealed en route. This is based on another teaching of Jesus, "Whoever has my commandments and obeys them, he is the one who loves me. He who loves me will be loved by my Father, and I too will love him and show myself to him"

(John 14:21). Obedience is evidence of our love. We know that Jesus loved us first (John 3:16; Rom. 5:8; 1 John 4:19). The natural response, Jesus says, is that we love him back through obedience, and when that happens he reciprocates by revealing more and more of himself to us.

Many people have considered going to Israel; they have studied the Bible and know a great deal about it. But until we stand on the Mount of Olives or before Golgotha, we really can't experience Israel. Many people have studied the Bible and considered following Jesus, but until we actually step out in obedience to him, we can't experience the transformation of our character. As we follow him, Jesus will reveal more about himself and about our mission day by day.

Identifying Your Strengths

As Jesus reveals our mission, we will be called on to use our gifts and talents for him. In recent years the discovery of one's gifts and talents has become a technical exercise. Thirty years ago there were no spiritual gifts tests or curriculums and very few psychological tools to measure our temperaments and create a personality profile. Yet I think people knew as much about their gifts and calling then as now. Jesus didn't have these tools and neither did his disciples.

While technical and psychological tools can be useful, there is a simpler way. Ask five of your friends to answer, "What am I good at? What strengths would you affirm in my life?" They will be the most accurate tool at your disposal, providing more valuable truth than money can buy. I asked this question of the elders of my former church. Of the six leadership issues listed as options, nine elders were unanimous on my top three strengths: (1) leadership/vision, (2) teaching, and (3) staff relations. That is a powerful statement when nine who know you well agree.

Another way to identify your gifts and talents is to ask, "Where is the fruit or impact of my work?" I like Paul's thinking on this, "I will not venture to speak of anything except what Christ has accomplished through me in leading the Gentiles to obey God by what I have said and done—by the powers of signs and miracles, through the power of the Spirit" (Rom. 15:18–19). Paul's calling was to take the gospel to the Gentiles, and all that mattered was the fruit of his work in which God had blessed his efforts.

Where has God blessed you; where is the fruit? The answer to that question is the key to finding your ministry "sweet spot." That is when your talent, God's timing, and his personal mission for you converge.

Paul knew where his gifts lay and sought more opportunities to use them: "It has always been my ambition to preach the gospel where Christ was not known, so that I would not be building on someone else's foundation" (Rom. 15:20). Paul's mission was to create new outposts for the kingdom; it was not to manage ministry. His calling matched his ambition, which fit his gifts.

Every active disciple of Jesus longs for the "sweet spot"—finding the mission that matches his or her gifts and talents. It is like a hitter on a hot streak, a stock broker who makes all the right decisions, or the concert pianist whose training and passion converge to create bliss. God condemns selfish ambition (James 3:14–16), but healthy ambition is essential to accomplishment. When you experience fruit, then go harder after that area. Fruitfulness is God's leading in our lives.

The Torment of the Daily

It would be grand if choosing the life was a one-time decision followed by ceaseless joy and success. Paul's life is evidence enough that while he knew he was on the right track, it was a tumultuous road (2 Cor. 4:8–16; 11:23–29). Yes, we do make a decision; we have chosen the life. We have repudiated nondiscipleship Christianity, and that is a firm, long-term commitment. But it must be lived out daily in the middle of temptation, weakness, illness, opposition, and the appearance of failure. Each day I must again say, "Yes, Jesus, I will follow you today. I will resist heading out on my own because I don't like the results you gave me yesterday. I won't bail out because others are abandoning ship. And I will follow you today even though I am depressed because I feel I have misread your mission for me." Choosing the life is an attitude, but it is in the daily living it out that the battle is waged.

Following with Doubt

I have always been ambitious. It is natural, it is who I am, and trying to deny it contorts my spirit. The challenge has been to allow my ambition to be used by God rather than letting selfish ambition influence my decisions.

Ever since my formative days at Oral Roberts University I have wanted to preach or teach. It was in Kenya in July of 1968 that God used me, and sixty-five people made a commitment to Christ at one time. (I must tell you that I have not matched that success since.) So as earlier modeled by Paul, I went in hot pursuit after that "sweet spot" moment. I played four years of basketball traveling the globe and telling others about Jesus, but the entire time I was preparing myself through reading and Bible study to become a teacher of the Word of God. I was very ambitious for it, and by the time I was thirty, I was pastoring a church and attending seminary.

The reason I pursued the pastorate was that it was the place I could teach and test my beliefs. If the purpose of the church is to make disciples, then it must work in the local church or it couldn't really be God's plan. I spent the next fourteen years learning how to do discipleship with ordinary people. I also began to write about my experiences and created a body of work that would give guidance to like-minded church leaders.

My writing created an interest in others and thus a seminar ministry began while I continued to pastor. Then I was confronted with a decision: Should I remain a pastor or pursue my passion for helping other churches? Many have done both at the same time, but I was led to spend my full time to create a church leadership training network named T-NET International. The next eight years were invested in its development. Throughout this entire period God was blessing the work and it was my ministry "sweet spot." It was also during those years that God gave me a distilled mission statement, "To help return the church to its disciple-making roots." And that remains my mission to this day.

I must confess, though, that I have followed that mission with some doubt. In 1997 I began to question whether I should remain as president of T-NET. It seemed that I had wandered off the "sweet spot," that my mission had changed. It was no longer about teaching the Word of God; it had become about raising funds and making deals so others could teach and influence. So I asked the board of directors for guidance, and they suggested I look at other options.

The option I chose was to return to the pastorate. I did so with fear and trembling, but I had always found it to be the most fertile ground for my writing. And this is crucial to my point about finding your missional "sweet spot" or to go hard after what God is blessing. I had to admit that the greatest impact of my life had been as a writer. So I wanted to be where the writing would be at its best. That place very often for me has been in ministry to a local congregation.

I have a close pastoral friend who predicted that about two or three years into it, I would kick myself down the street for returning to the rough and tumble of the local church. What I thought would happen at first did happen. The ministry went very well. The church grew a bit, and we completed a fantastic building project in which 95 percent of the pledges were paid. Optimism reigned.

Then it was as though a plague swept through the land. For nearly three years I experienced rejection at a gut-wrenching level. Scores of people left the church, and some of the staff were subversive in their behavior and did a great deal of damage. My pastoring skills were rusty, and I was ministering mostly out of my head, without communicating from my heart. I strongly questioned my decision to be a pastor.

This is why Jesus said we have to deny ourselves and take up our cross daily (Luke 9:23). Every single day I had to affirm my commitment to follow rather than lead, to stay, not run, to swallow my pride and listen to the critics. But the biggest issue of all was my belief that I had misread God's leading in my life, that I had bailed on T-NET, and this is what you get when you screw up.

Had I violated Paul's instructions to pursue my ambition, the mission that God has placed in my heart? There was very little fruit; most of what I saw was waste. I had wasted good years that now seemed more precious. I had wasted relationships that took me years to develop. Worst of all, I was now four years behind on my mission. But following Jesus has many dimensions, and God has every right to overrule our logic and understanding of his Word and principles.

When I cried out to Jesus in my despair, asking him to forgive me for bailing on my mission, he said, "Bill, stay right where you are. Remember, I'm leading. You are my servant; your reputation, your success is not your concern. You have no greater right to a good reputation than I had. I am building my church; it doesn't depend on you. I have your future in my hands. You have made mistakes, but returning to pastoring wasn't one of them. I have you here for a reason. I will let you know when it is time to go." It wasn't an audible voice, but over a period of weeks this message became clear, and I know it was from Jesus. That is when it all changed for me. I laid my dreams, ambitions, and books at his feet and gave in.

We are called to follow God's leading. When our mission fails to produce fruit, we still must follow and submit, because he is doing something that will help us be even more fruitful in the future. Sometimes we think the fruit is about us, our ideas, and our abilities. Then God must prune it from our lives. So as we take up our cross and choose daily to follow him, there may be some days, weeks, even months when we will lack success. But if we stay behind him and under him, we will find something far greater than the cost of discipleship.

Gaining Your Soul

Life is full of paradoxes, and I have found that golf is one of them. In football or basketball, anger and adrenaline can improve your game. But it doesn't work that way with golf. The paradox is if you want to hit the ball further, you have to swing easy and smooth. If you want the ball to go left, hit it to the right. If you want it to go right, hit it to the left.

God has created a paradox that is counterintuitive to the human condition. It has to do with gaining our souls or, to put it another way, finding everything we really want.

God's Paradox

If you want to save your life, to put your agenda first and control conditions and results, then you will lose your life. Gaining and losing in this context is about the basic choice of salvation. Notice that Jesus defines salvation not in terms of doctrine but in terms of action. This is because faith is action based on belief. So belief as defined by Jesus is following, self-denial, taking up our cross daily, and obeying him. This does not violate contemporary concepts of grace; it simply defines the nature of faith.

Jesus' statement is clear, "For whoever wants to save his life will lose it" (Luke 9:24). The most natural impulse is to set your goal, develop a plan, and go after it. This, however, will backfire because if we insist on directing our own lives, we will never enter into the joy and fulfillment of God's dream for us. It is clearly stated that God has a dream for us that makes our dreams ho-hum and drab. "For we are God's workmanship, created in Christ Jesus to do good works, which God prepared in advance for us to do" (Eph. 2:10).

The reason for following rather than leading is that Jesus knows where we need to go. Just as he promised to prepare a place in heaven for us (John 14:1–3), he has prepared a life for us right now that is full of meaning and purpose. When we try to control it, we do not have enough wisdom or knowledge to find that ministry "sweet spot."

Hold your life loosely. Forget yourself, follow him, and let him take you where you need to go. Lose yourself in the mission; that is the joyful wonderland of his plan for every follower. If you have plans and strategies that haven't worked and show no sign of God's blessing, then retreat to the surety of his leadership. I often pray, "Lord I am your servant. I will follow you even if it is into apparent failure. I have no rights to success as I define it or as the church defines it or as my culture defines it. I am only interested in pleasing you and being successful as you define it."

You might protest that this seems like abdication of responsibility, but I don't agree. The first responsibility of a servant is to follow and to do his master's will. Jesus tells me to lose my life in the mission, to relinquish control of my life to him. When I do this, and only when I do this, will I find all that I have ever wanted. The true rewards are in finding my life.

The Rewards

When we answer the call to the Society of Jesus, that special order of disciples who follow him seriously, there are great rewards. There is the joy of knowing that our lives are in a bull's eye with God's. It is comforting to know that one day we will hear what every servant desires: "Well done, my good and faithful servant." We can be inspired by the words Paul issued near the end of his life,

> For I am already being poured out like a drink offering, and the time has come for my departure. I have fought the good fight, I have finished the race, I have kept the faith. Now there is in store for me the crown of righteousness, which the Lord, the righteous Judge, will award to me on that day.
>
> 2 Timothy 4:6–8

It is every disciple's dream to live a life that has great meaning and fulfillment. But that life does not come to those who drift about as immature converts. It belongs only to those who choose the life, the life of transformational discipleship. God is raising up men and women all over America who are hungry for God. He is raising up leaders who want to be the revolutionaries that Christ intended us to be when he told us to make disciples and teach them everything that Christ commanded. But first we must teach ourselves what Christ commanded; first we must commit to allowing him to form our spirits. We must make that the most important and exclusive task of all. When passion and power return to the leaders of the church, then the revolution can begin.

4

THE HABITS
OF THE LIFE

Widespread transformation of character through
wisely disciplined discipleship to Christ can transform our world. It can disarm the structural evils
that have always dominated humankind and now
threaten to destroy the world.[1]

—Dallas Willard

Discipleship is about transformation of character. It is
about Christ being formed in us.[2] My thesis is in agreement with Willard: When the church goes deep, we get real
transformation; there will be revolution; there will be revival;
there will be reproduction; and there will be multiplication. The

1. Dallas Willard, *The Spirit of the Disciplines* (San Francisco: Harper & Row, 1988), xi.
2. *Formed* or *morphe* is the root word employed in Romans 8:29; 12:2; Galatians 4:19.

mother lode for the Great Commission is depth, a deepen-
ing of evangelical character. Since we lead from our character,
our influence will be greater with a deepened, more Christlike
character.

This is where the spiritual formation movement comes in. It
has now emerged from behind the walls of monasteries and out
of the neoorthodox seminary classrooms to become a force in
the mainstream. It brings a rich history of great contemplative
writers, scholarship, and an emphasis on spiritual disciplines. The
bottom line for transformation is that character is developed
supernaturally through habits. And those habits are acquired
through discipline in the context of a faith community. In fact,
the effect of the disciplines is tested in community. The development of love, for example, is tested when I am called to love
someone who does not love me. Now I just said a mouthful; it
will take me several pages to unpack it.

THE HABITS ARE ALREADY PRESCRIBED

The habits or spiritual disciplines have a rich history. There
are anywhere from twelve to twenty depending on the source.[3]
Examples are Bible reading, meditating, memorization, prayer,
worship, evangelism, service, stewardship, fasting, silence, solitude, journaling, submission, and frugality. The normal evangelical pattern has been Bible reading, memorization, prayer,
worship, evangelism, service, and stewardship.[4]

The method of teaching these disciplines, however, has not
helped the disciple develop them as habits of the heart. The

3. See Richard Foster, *Celebration of Discipline* (San Francisco: Harper & Row, 1978);
Dallas Willard, *The Spirit of the Disciplines*; or Don Whitney, *Disciplines for the Christian Life*
(Colorado Springs: NavPress, 1983). There is agreement on the core disciplines such as
Bible intake, meditation on Scripture, prayer, worship, fasting, frugality, silence, solitude,
and stewardship.

4. See Richard Foster, *Celebration of Discipline*. Foster defines and explains each major
spiritual discipline. It is not part of my writing mission to duplicate the fine work Foster
has already provided.

method far too often has been a pulpit exhortation with an offer of joining a class or small group. But in all honesty, the actual practice has been left up to the individual to make it on his or her own. Any attempt to get closer or to ask for more is when the trouble starts because people are naturally self-protective. We put up barriers; we want transformation without change and character development without pain.

Yet submission, humility, and vulnerability are essential prerequisites to transformation. Submission to God, humility with others, and vulnerability means openness to the influence of others. The needed dynamic goes back to the five characteristics of first-century discipleship (see chapter 1). Characteristics 1 and 5 have been missing in the church, so the chance of the disciplines actually becoming habits is slim. Number 1 is submitting to at least one other person who teaches you how to follow Jesus. We will discuss submission in chapter 8, but we are talking about much more than agreeing to meet with someone and fill out a Bible study book. Characteristic 5 is the expectation that once trained you will go find your own disciples. Regardless of the success by churches of getting large numbers of members into small groups or personal mentoring, it all comes down to the strong presence of loving accountability and expected reproduction. All else is preaching to the choir and talking to ourselves, which isn't disciple making at all; it is religious activity without transformation. If we want to transform culture as Dallas Willard suggests at the beginning of this chapter, we must make disciples where the unbeliever lives. We can't stay in the church and wait for them to walk in; they aren't coming.

WHY PRACTICE SPIRITUAL DISCIPLINES?

According to Dallas Willard, "The spiritual disciplines are essential to the deliverance of human beings from the concrete power of sin."[5] The interplay between discipline and disciple is

5. Dallas Willard, *The Spirit of the Disciplines*, 10.

not without importance. John Ortberg says, "Disciplined people can do the right thing at the right time in the right way for the right reason."[6] The practice of the disciplines develops habits of the heart that make a disciple more capable of answering the call of God on his or her life.

When Jesus asked Peter, James, and John to wait and pray nearby while he wrestled with his Father, three times they went to sleep. That was when he spoke those most penetrating words, "The spirit is willing, but the flesh is weak" (Matt. 26:41). This episode answers why we need to practice the disciplines. Jesus was telling them that by participating in a certain type of action—staying awake and being in prayer—they would be able to reach a quality of spiritual strength that would be impossible without it. We need the spiritual disciplines not to accentuate our strengths but to address our weaknesses.

Think about the contrast in the disciples once they were empowered by the Holy Spirit. In the garden they couldn't stay awake and pray for a few minutes, yet later they sustained the discipline for ten days (Acts 1). The filling of the Holy Spirit is essential, because the Spirit of the disciplines is the Holy Spirit.[7] But there is more to it than just the filling of the Spirit. There are too many Spirit-filled followers who are undisciplined, untrained, underused, and ineffective. Spirit filling is about the heart's intention; it gives a person the desire to be trained, but desire doesn't do the training.

THE DISCIPLINES ARE JUST TOOLS

The disciplines have no value in and of themselves. If the idea is to produce depth for depth's sake, it is self-indulgent and births pride, the king of sins. It reminds me of body building. Young men and women dedicate themselves to a physical regimen of exercise and diet that is impressive. Many enter body-building

6. John Ortberg, *The Life You've Always Wanted* (Grand Rapids: Zondervan, 1997), 55.
7. This is the reason Dallas Willard titled his 1988 classic *The Spirit of the Disciplines.*

competitions; they prance about a stage and display their well oiled sculpted bodies. But what can their bodies do that a normal body can't do? Very little that is important. For disciples to exercise and create impressive spiritual muscles simply for display is a stench in God's nostrils. "Look at how long I pray or how much I fast. God speaks to me a lot. I give a great deal. Look at my big fat journal." No self-respecting disciple would be so blatant, but in very subtle ways it comes out. There is no virtue in spiritual exercise without a reason, and that reason is the Great Commission; it is, as we have already considered, losing ourselves in the mission (Luke 9:23–25).

The aim and substance of following Jesus is not prayer, Bible study, or meditation. The role of these spiritual disciplines is to serve the greater purpose of knowing God. They are to help us develop an intimacy with God and a fitness for service. In fact, they accentuate our weakness and need for character development. Spiritual disciplines are to transformation what calisthenics are to sport.[8] Calisthenics have been around a long time, and every sports team does them: push-ups, jumping jacks, leg lifts, sit-ups, and of course everyone's favorite, pull-ups. I must say I was never very good at calisthenics. If making the basketball team was based on my calisthenic ability, my trophy case would be empty. My college scholarship and the many awards I won would be nonexistent. The coaches used to laugh at me because I could only do one pull-up, just twenty-five push-ups, and that was in my prime. But that wasn't the point; the calisthenics only helped condition my body so when I ran out on the court, I could use my gifts.

The practice of the disciplines is essential for transformation, so we must address the aversion the church populace has to the stereotypical image of spiritual exercise. We are faced with a church full of gifted people with a desire to serve who are not conditioned and are unprepared to serve well.

8. John Ortberg, *The Life You've Always Wanted*, 49.

THE SPIRITUAL DISCIPLINES WORK INDIRECTLY

Spiritual exercise works much like physical exercise. I have exercised most of my life; in fact, I'm addicted to it. It has changed over the years based on my abilities, but it is an integral part of my well-being. Exercise sets into motion a series of positive events inside the body. The heart rate increases which increases blood flow. The vessels and arteries open wider. Oxygen flows stronger. The heart gets stronger. The muscles maintain their strength. The entire cardiovascular system is enhanced. It makes it possible for me to still play basketball, walk long distances, lift my luggage into overhead compartments without help, play with my grandson, and lift and carry things for my wife.

Similarly, spiritual exercise sets into motion a series of positive events that strengthen and transform one's character. The Scriptures say we are being transformed "by the renewing of [our] mind" (Rom. 12:2), and we "are being tranformed into [the Lord's] likeness (2 Cor. 3:18). "Though outwardly we are wasting away, yet inwardly we are being renewed day by day" (2 Cor. 4:16). It is a mystery how reading, memorizing, and meditating on the Scripture can transform the mind and then behavior, but they do. The spiritual disciplines transform the mind and train us for everything we need to do (see 1 Tim. 4:6–7; 2 Tim. 3:17; Heb. 5:14; 12:11). Character is formed by the Holy Spirit, and the disciplines are the tools. They are essential because we know Jesus practiced them, and so did his followers.

There is no slavery that can compare to the slavery of ingrained habits of sin. Willpower is no defense against the careless word, the unguarded moment. It has to be the supernatural work of the Holy Spirit in combination with our wills.

Three principles govern the practice of the disciplines. We now turn our attention to them.

1. THE GOAL IS GODLINESS

The Spirit of God has been planted in us and is the source of our motivation. The desire to be like Jesus is "factory installed" by the Holy Spirit at the moment of spiritual birth. There is a perpetual hunger for holiness, to be different like Jesus is different.[9] Paul puts it in direct terms: *"Train yourselves to be godly"* (1 Tim. 4:7, emphasis added). Sounds like work, doesn't it? There are so many disciplines, how can one practice fifteen-plus disciplines simultaneously? The answer is you can't and you shouldn't. I like Eugene Peterson's image; he likened the disciplines to a set of garden tools. He saw the soil of a garden as the human soul, the rain and sunshine as the staple disciplines such as interaction with the Scriptures and prayer. The other tools are over in the shed, used when it's time to till, weed, plant, or do some other task. The disciple has fasting, solitude, worship, journaling, and others in the tool shed, stored for when needed. There are times when extended times of prayer and fasting are needed.[10] Just yesterday my wife spent a day in intense prayer, solitude, listening, and fasting. It was just something she needed to nourish her soul. So she pulled four tools out of the spiritual disciplines shed. So there is no need to be intimidated by the number of disciplines available any more than we are by the one hundred television channels at our fingertips.

The Road to Godliness Is One of Discipline

The word *train* comes from *gumnaze*, from which we derive *gymnastics* and *gymnasium*.[11] It is a word dripping with sweat; it is out of breath and its muscles are burning. It seems antithetical

9. *Holiness* comes from the root word *hagios*. It can be translated "saint," "holy," "set apart." It really means "different." God is different; his attributes make him unique. Another way of saying "Holy, Holy, Holy" is "different, different, different." This rescues holiness from a legalistic image of dark, plain clothes—a boring life without joy.

10. Eugene Peterson, *Under the Unpredictable Plant: An Exploration in Vocational Holiness* (Grand Rapids: Eerdmans, 1992), 110.

11. *Gumnaze* is found in Hebrews 5:14; 12:11; 2 Peter 2:14.

to everything Christian or at least the contemporary evangelical image of Christian growth. It is so easy to go to extremes, in our thinking and in our doing. One of those extremes has been the *de facto* belief that grace is opposed to effort. There is a resistance to spiritual disciplines in the body of Christ by those who equate effort with earning grace points with God. This may be part of a negative reflex to effort as being dead works and contrary to justification by faith. There is great discomfort with the idea that spiritual disciplines are necessary and part of what it means to believe in Christ. Somehow the self-denial Jesus described as basic to faith and following him has disappeared from the salvation equation.

The disciplining of one's natural impulses is central to the teaching of the Scriptures, but it has been cast aside by most. Frankly, a lot of the resistance comes from a reaction to the monastic movement and its overcooking or even its malpractice of the spiritual disciplines.[12] There is also a resistance by evangelicals to Catholic teaching and liberal theology that has been the home for the spiritual disciplines for the last few hundred years. The interesting development of the last ten years is the emergence of a very healthy spirituality from those traditions. The malpractice of the disciplines is when the earning or maintaining of salvation is implied, when somehow the believer thinks that God will love him more or lavish him with praise for his effort, when the disciplines dominate the disciple's life and obstructs or replaces intimacy with God, and most importantly when the disciplines become a mission that replaces the Great Commission.

God Is Opposed to Earning but Encourages Effort

I would agree that God is opposed to earning salvation through the practice of any set of disciplines. *But I would strongly suggest that he is not opposed to effort.* In fact, some of the great passages in the New

12. A fuller treatment of the resistance to spiritual disciplines and their connection to the monastic movement can be found in Dallas Willard, *The Spirit of the Disciplines*, 130–54.

Testament extol effort (see I Cor. 9:24–27; 2 Cor. 11:23–29; Gal. 4:19; Phil. 3:9–16; Col. 1:28–30; 2 Tim. 2:1–11; Heb. 5:11–13). The road to godliness is one of discipline, and discipline doesn't come naturally to most. This is why we seldom go it alone, in isolation from a community of those who help care for our souls.

Don't Go It Alone

Why are there workout clubs or packs of men and women running together? Not only are we social beings, we also need encouragement when discipline is involved. I saw a television report recently that 70 percent of Americans do not exercise. Of the 30 percent who do exercise, less than 10 percent exercise alone. These people are very disciplined and don't need anyone. The remaining 90 percent of people who exercise do so because of accountability or encouragement from a friend.

Attachment to at least one other person is absolutely essential. I hardly know a soul who has made significant breakthroughs without the help of friends. Many people have said, "I'm going to go deep with God," but unless they submit to the help of others, it is not likely to happen apart from suffering. Going deep is not learning all the details of the Hebrew and Greek Bible; it is returning good for evil, encouraging your spouse when you want to criticize, responding to the needs around us. The help of others is part of the road of discipline that makes transformation into godliness possible. Now for the second principle.

2. THE IMPORTANCE OF PRACTICE

I have practiced a lot of things in my life. Some of the practice paid off, some did not. I stayed at the practice that paid off and quit the practice that didn't. I was determined and persistent in basketball, but after a year I quit the piano. I learned that being six-foot-four was more useful on the court than at the keyboard. I practiced preaching and writing like a physician practices medicine. It was required that I reach a necessary level of competence before I was able to practice on others. The reason for practice is so that you will do things automatically the same way every time.

A passage on effort explains the relationship of practice to training: "We have much to say about this, but it is hard to explain because you are slow to learn. In fact, though by this time you ought to be teachers, you need someone to teach you the elementary truths of God's word all over again. You need milk, not solid food!" (Hebrews 5:11–12).

The Undiscipled Disciples

Notice the indictment made by the writer to the Hebrews: "*Though by this time you ought to be teachers,* you need someone to teach you the elementary truths of God's word all over again" (Heb. 5:12, emphasis added). The cost of discipleship is meager when compared to the cost of nondiscipleship.[13] The church is seriously debilitated by the belief that the test of salvation is doctrinal rather than behavioral. So we could have one segment of our congregations that are engaged in church activity but have not repented of their sin and have decided not to follow Jesus. I think it is clear that Jesus defined belief as following him (see Luke 9:23–25). Then there is a second group that have truly repented and in good faith are following Jesus, but what it means to follow Jesus has been reduced to church attendance, financial giving, and serving on a board or committee. This doesn't happen with a conscious choice; it happens by custom and church culture. This second group has not been challenged to "choose the life." There is no intentional discipleship focused on internal transformation. So you have two groups, the first being religious without transformation and the second truly saved but under-challenged and hung out to dry. This second group is what I call

13. See Bill Hull, *High Commitment in a Low Commitment World* (Grand Rapids: Revell, 1995); and Dallas Willard, *The Spirit of the Disciplines* (San Francisco: Harper & Row, 1988), appendix 1.

undiscipled disciples. And the body of Christ is paying a huge price because of them, the high cost of nondiscipleship.

Undiscipled disciples are not new; they were even present in the early church. But it is sad that we have let the status of un-discipled disciple become a normal condition. It is the common cold of the church, and we haven't found a cure, so we accept it as a fact of life.

The High Cost of Nondiscipleship

Nondiscipleship Christianity is the elephant in the room. We have denied it exists; we have thrown a large table cloth over it and called it a coffee table. It has cost us a vibrant church. It has cost us the fulfillment of the Great Commission. We feed the elephant, and he stays strong and dominant. What does he eat? His favorite dish is that everyone's commitment level is acceptable; therefore, everyone deserves the same investment of time and resources. This always comes with a side dish of meeting the demands of the immature and the passive-aggressive underachievers. For dessert, he likes to keep leaders occupied arbitrating conflict among those vying for power born of their pathology. In this milieu people are not expected to take the kingdom of God to work and make disciples. There is just no time and energy left for that. The majority of time and effort is consumed in keeping the elephant well fed. Therefore, there is less joy, passion, and fruitfulness. The cost is so high because lives are wasted, and life-changing experiences are left on the shelf.

The pastor spends his best time and energy trying to satisfy the prevailing desires of the congregation. I know how hard it is to stay on course and be pure in philosophy and strategy. But the nondiscipleship Christianity that we have accepted is a leadership problem. The solution is that leaders must model what they believe their followers should do. And it will take a group of tightly knit leaders who are willing to take a lot of criticism in order to starve the elephant and feed their souls.

The enemy strategy is to keep us away from the habits of the heart that will develop Christ's character in his people. The Great Commission is more about depth than strategy. It is about a revolution of character transformation.[14]

The indictment of the Hebrews is that they have failed to be proponents for the kingdom of God. Instead, they have stagnated, lost their passion, and will have to be recycled. Reminding believers that we are way behind is considered rude and in bad form. But there is a place for it since it is done so often in Scripture. The original recipients of the book of Hebrews had formed bad habits. Their spiritual formation was actually a malformation of passivity and a retreat from making disciples themselves. Yet reproduction is a clear expectation of discipleship.[15]

In my church we once acquired a study of the religious practices of residents within a seven-mile radius of our church. About 48 percent or six hundred thousand residents said they practiced no faith of any kind. I asked our congregation if they each had a personal plan to reach the nearly 50 percent of people living around them who were in need of Christ. Many in our congregation are faithful to speak of their faith and take a stand for their beliefs. But I wondered out loud to them why we haven't done more to teach others. I recalled that old hymn, "Bring in the Sheaves," which defines our mission so simply: "we shall come rejoicing, bring in the sheaves." Trained teachers go out and bring in those they have taught.

This is God's plan for his church, because everyone can do it. He doesn't indict us for a lack of talent or charisma, only for not living up to the potential that God has planted in us. All of this will require training; that training is accomplished through practice. That training begins with a way of thinking and then with a way of doing. The expectation that we are each to take

14. Transformation qualifies us to be ambassadors, to take the message to others (2 Cor. 5:17–21).

15. The fifth of the five characteristics of first-century discipleship was the making of new disciples. This is the lost art of the modern discipleship movement. May we rediscover it.

responsibility to reach others and bring them into the community of faith is a learning process. Believe me, the majority of your church thinks it is the church staff's job to bring new people in through excellent programs and preaching. This will require some serious unlearning, the elimination of bad habits and the acquisition of good ones.

The Mature Are Trained by Practice

Hebrews 5:14 says, "But solid food is for the mature, who by constant use have trained themselves to distinguish good from evil." Maturity is about "constant use," and constant use means repetition, what we call practice, and that requires discipline. Real change takes time while new habits are set in place. There can be terrific struggles that go on inside of us as the battle rages. The devil Screwtape describes it from the other point of view in C. S. Lewis's *Screwtape Letters*: "There is no need to despair; hundreds of these adult converts have been reclaimed after a brief sojourn in the Enemy's camp and are now with us. All the *habits* of the patient, both mental and bodily, are still in our favour."[16]

If a new habit isn't formed, change is temporary. That seems to be the modus operandi for most people. The church is moved most often by inspiration, and that is needed and good. God moves us to action through our minds and emotions. But when the inspirational moment is our base, the staple of our spiritual diet, we will slip back into the same habits as before, and the advance of the kingdom must once again be delayed.

Body and Soul

We cannot separate the body from the transformation process. Paul was clear about this when he told us "offer the parts of your body to him as instruments of righteousness. For sin shall not

16. C. S. Lewis, *The Screwtape Letters* (New York: Macmillan, 1962), 11.

be your master, because you are not under law, but under grace" (Rom. 6:13–14).

This is one of those moments in a book when the author must state how what he is saying is different or crucial: *The key to inner transformation is making the spiritual disciplines habit forming.* Being trained is a product of practice. These habits actually change the composition of the soul. Prayer, solitude, and fasting can break the chains of lust or sexual perversion. The discipline of worship can release one from constant preoccupation with self. Keeping a prayer journal can replace depression with joy, bitterness with forgiveness. The disciplines are about submission of the body, submission of the will, the consistent submission of life's appetites to the lordship of Christ. It's not about information but formation, of our spirits and the attitudes and actions that come from it. We practice them until they become second nature, until we enjoy his presence more than television or an evening with friends.

Practicing the disciplines creates a new awareness in our souls of something that needs to be changed. Let's say God is impressing on me the importance of loving those I find irritating. To love like he loved is to find ways to get through to others so they experience love. God has a way of bringing people into our lives that really get under our skin. One such person is in my life right now. The problem is that I am to love this person as Christ loved me; so I have fallen short of that commitment. Now the discipline is to step toward this person and find ways to communicate love and acceptance. That is how discipline changes character.

3. PERSEVERANCE MAKES TRANSFORMATION A REALITY

Everyone knows that practice plus enough time equals a new habit. The difference between talented people and trained people is immense. There are many gifted people who do not fulfill their potential because they will not train. They don't keep it up long enough for it to become a powerful force. The power of habit is that it takes what once was hard and awkward and makes it natural and easy.

In my mid-teens I was a rising basketball star. I had some natural talent, but I wasn't the most talented. I found that I was not blessed with great jumping ability, and bigger, quicker players could block my shot. It was then that I determined to learn the hook shot. I was determined not only to learn the hook shot but to master it with both hands. There is a special technique that must be followed, and I first practiced it with my right hand. Within a few weeks I had mastered the right-hand hook. It took me months to master it with my left hand. When I was comfortable and confident in the back yard, I planned to debut it during a game. The real test is when people are guarding you in the heat of competition. I started with the right, and it went in; then I faked my opponent and hooked with the left, and it went in. Now they didn't know if I was going to drive to the basket, pull up and knock down the jumper, use a fade-away jumper, or go down low and hook right or left. This made me a very good offensive player and scoring became easy for me. I spent many days and weeks in mind-numbing repetition before I got it. But when I made that first lefty hook on a surprised defender, it was all worth it. I was filled with delight at how easy it seemed, and I didn't have to think about it. It just came naturally in the moment; that is what the spiritual disciplines are to do.

God has prescribed memorization of Scripture. When in the middle of a tough battle we recall the verse and it keeps us from sin, that discipline has served us so we can serve him.

Giving God a Chance

Paul once again provides the thinking: "Do not be deceived: God cannot be mocked. People reap what they sow. Those who sow to please their sinful nature, from that nature will reap destruction; those who sow to please the Spirit, from that Spirit will reap eternal life. *Let us not become weary in doing good, for at the proper time we will reap a harvest if we do not give up*" (paraphrase of Gal. 6:7–9).

A decision to follow Jesus includes the prioritizing of my actions. My intention then is to "sow to the Spirit." I am to deny self by engaging God through his prescribed disciplines with the confidence that the process will set into motion inner transformation. "Sowing to the sinful nature" is to indulge my appetites and drift into a life of nondiscipleship.

Don't Become Weary

Change is possible only when perseverance is present. Perseverance itself is a spiritual discipline. I wasn't as talented as other athletes, but I went further because I practiced longer and harder. As a schoolboy I played basketball every day, year round from the time I was fourteen until twenty-one. I played in back yards, alleys, school yards, gymnasiums, and in the winter in converted haylofts that housed basketball courts.

Most people lose perseverance when they lose sight of their goal. My goal was simple. My mother made $39.00 a week, and unless I was good enough to get a basketball scholarship to a university, I was going into the Army and to Viet Nam. I had made this commitment when I was fired from my newspaper route. The paper manager came to my home to confront me about my unpaid bill and customer complaints. It was all true; I had spent my bill and I had missed customers. The craggy old guy, around forty, challenged me: "What are you going to do with your life? You're a disaster!" I looked him straight in the eye and said, "I'm going to college on a basketball scholarship." He screwed up his face and threw up his hands. "That's a laugh," he said and walked out the door. I was fourteen years old back then, and I dedicated myself to practice the disciplines of basketball. Four years later I walked onto the college campus, and I had already paid the bill. I paid with four years of perseverance. I was trained, and they now would pay me to use my skills.

I was able to keep focused on my goal because it was clear and concrete. But very often spiritual goals are ethereal and hard to grasp. The antidote for weariness is keeping the vision in mind and staying at the disciplines that you deeply believe will pay off one day. Paul tells us we will reap a great harvest if we don't give up. There will be days when prayer is emotional drudgery, when silence leads to unplanned naps and listening prayer to mental rabbit trails. It is during those times that we hang our hope on the belief that it will pay off. Perseverance has created greatness much more than talent ever has or will. Greatness is a character quality that can only be developed when progress can't be seen.

I remember sending to a catalogue company for leg weights that I could wear in order to increase my vertical jump. I was so excited when they arrived, I ripped open the box, strapped them on, and headed for the garage. Day after day I would hold a barbell of weights on my shoulders and with the weights strapped to my ankles I would do jumping scissors, twenty-five repetitions, followed by twenty-five more and twenty-five more. It hurt as my feet pounded into cinder floor in that old window-less garage. After thirty minutes with sweat pouring off of me, I would run out into my back yard to see if I could jump higher. Weeks went by, and I could not really tell if it was working, but I kept it up because I believed it would work, and my vision was clear: I needed to jump higher in order to go to college and not Viet Nam. After a few months I noticed that I was stronger and getting two or three inches higher. I never became a great leaper, but I was able to play much better because I did this exercise.

God tells us to pray, fast, and be silent before him, to practice solitude, worship, and stewardship, and to submit to others. If we follow these disciplines faithfully, they will change us.

Training Instead of Trying

The theme that dominates this entire discussion of transformation is the importance of training. Paul spoke of training ourselves to be godly (1 Tim. 4:7); the writer to the Hebrews told us that constant use or practice leads to someone who is trained (Heb. 5:14). Paul pointed out to Timothy that Scriptures provide the primary means for the training in righteousness needed so that every person will be thoroughly equipped to do every good work (2 Tim. 3:16–17). Training to be godly is very different from trying to be godly. Trying to be godly doesn't work, training does.

I could challenge my church members to run seven miles. We could gather in front of the church and run together so we could encourage one another. I could give an inspirational message that would fire them up so they would be brimming over with desire to run the seven miles. But almost no one could run seven miles. There would be very courageous efforts as many would extend themselves beyond what they should to reach the goal. But the first aid station and recovery tent would be filled with the injured and the sick. A few people would make it, but it wouldn't be a matter of age or necessarily body strength. Those who would finish would be those who had already been running as a way of life.

Trying to be godly without training can be just as injurious to the spirit as trying to run seven miles without proper training can be to the body. I think Christians should stop trying to be godly and start practicing the disciplines that form pathways to the heart of God and transform us into his likeness.

The distinction between trying and training is revolutionary. So many resist effort and discipline because it seems like an external effort to gain an internal change. But when I am training, change occurs not because I am straining to make something happen but because I am doing what God prescribed. Training via disciplined practice is how genuine freedom is attained. It is how Jesus' yoke is easy and light.

The spiritual disciplines are a systematization and extension of practices followed by Jesus and his earliest followers. They have been practiced throughout history by followers of Jesus. They are the habits of the life that enable us to accomplish what we cannot do by direct effort.

ANSWER THE CALL

We have documented the need for the life in chapter 2. The call to the life is clear from chapter 3. The habits of the life are the means to answering the call. Yet because of the continuing problem of weak and shallow character, we are not on schedule to the fulfillment of the Great Commission. The cure is to answer the call to the life because faith is more than doctrinal assent it is action; it is actually following Jesus. The means, then, to this character revolution is transformation by training in the prescribed disciplines. As these habits become second nature they set into motion a supernatural change.

Now we move into the inner workings of this transformation. Don't shrink back from what lies before you in this exhortation; read on. Don't become weary; there is a great payoff waiting for you. I love what G. K. Chesterton said about Christianity, "Christianity has not so much been tried and found wanting, as it has been found difficult and not tried."[17] My adaptation is, "Discipleship/spiritual formation has not been tried and found wanting, as it has been found difficult and not tried."

17. G. K. Chesterton, *What's Wrong with the World* (Ft. Collins, Colo.: Ignatius, 1994), chap. 5.

5

THE INNER WORKINGS OF THE LIFE

How Character Is Formed

Many churched people have a spiritual life that's like a car, sputtering down the highway, coughing and jerking, red engine lights flashing. The driver's solution is to beat a fist on the dashboard until the warning lights quit flashing. He or she motors on, believing that eliminating the warning signs is the same as fixing the problem. This is how most Christians are taught to treat the spiritual predicaments in which they find themselves . . . try harder, read the Bible more, pound on the spiritual dashboard until the warnings cease. Something is wrong with the engine—the machinery of faith, the *inner workings* are seriously impaired.[1]

—Judith Hougen, emphasis added

1. Judith Hougen, *Transformed into Fire* (Grand Rapids: Kregel, 2003), 20.

W hat is under the hood? What does my spiritual engine look like? Nondiscipleship Christianity is sputtering along the road, and the warning lights are on. The main warning light reads "lack of character." This lack is the primary reason for the superficial nature of today's believers.

It is painfully obvious that we have overlooked the single most important element for fulfilling the Great Commission. It seems we have been so busy trying to reach the world that there has been no time to focus on being like Jesus. So we haven't reached the world, and we aren't very much like Jesus. Since the Great Commission is driven by depth more than strategy, the mission of the church has been greatly weakened. Depth means passion; it means connection to God. Depth gives credibility that following Jesus matters as our immaterial nature is transformed into the characteristics of Christ—more compassion than detachment, more humility than hubris, less comparison and more unity.

Jesus had an impact because of who he was and how he touched people. Why should it be any different with us? Through the practice of the spiritual disciplines, we can experience a change in character.

The purpose of physical exercise is health; it sets into motion natural forces that strengthen the body. Spiritual exercises set into motion an inner working of the Holy Spirit. But the spiritual calisthenics must have the right intention: to have one's entire immaterial nature be conformed to the image of Christ. This is a love response on the disciple's part to please his God and be able to answer the call on his life.

God works inside out as we pray, meditate, fast, record our thoughts, or give of our resources. Whatever we do in word or deed, we do in the name of Jesus (Col. 3:17). Through these spiritual exercises our character—our resource for action, a combination of intentions, habits, feelings, beliefs, and actions—is changed to be more like Christ.

BEING LIKE BOBBY

When I was a young boy, I hadn't yet thought about becoming more like Christ, but I did want to be like Bobby Logan. Bobby was my alter ego as a boy. He existed only in my mind, but he dominated my life. Bobby could hit like Mickey Mantle, jump like Bill Russell, and quarterback like Johnny Unitas. And he always came through in the clutch by scoring the winning touchdown or dropping the thirty-footer at the buzzer. He was great at all sports, but his best sport was basketball. No one had the quickness, the vertical leap, the shooting eye, and the competitive fire to match Bobby.

Bobby Logan was my imaginary vision of a great athlete. I was inspired to be like Bobby, and it made a huge difference in my life. But as I developed my own persona and success, Bobby faded into the background. The only thing Bobby did was sports; he didn't go to school or have parents. He didn't have a girlfriend or a house. Bobby never grew up, and eventually he went on to enter into another little dreamer's thoughts.

Now my dreams are spiritual; I want to be like Jesus. Bobby was not real; Jesus is. I couldn't really be as good as Bobby, and I can't become like Jesus in that he is God. But I can take on Jesus' character, and his thoughts, his feelings, and his values can become mine. Just as those hours and hours of practice transformed my athletic life, the time I spend practicing the spiritual disciplines can transform my inner person. It is time to go beyond agreement that being like Jesus is a good thing and invest in the process.

WHAT WE ARE LIKE INSIDE

There has been much debate as to how to label our immaterial nature. Some say we are split into three parts: body, spirit, and emotions. Others contend that we are just two parts: body and spirit. I don't think anyone can know this for sure; it is all about interpretation of the various words used by biblical writers.[2] I have chosen six words that are used to describe what is happening inside a person.

Will: the power to initiate/decide (1 Cor. 7:37)

Spirit: that part of us that is distinct from the body (1 Cor. 2:9–16)

Heart: the core or center of a person (Col. 3:1)

Feelings: emotions, sensations (Eph. 4:31)

Conscience: an inner knowing of right and wrong (1 Peter 3:16)

Mind: the rational center of our being (Rom. 12:2)

These terms describe what is happening in the context of the biblical passages listed. When the writer speaks of choice he uses will, if his focus is total commitment he would employ heart, if referring to anger or malice, he would be describing feelings. If one is struggling with right and wrong, it would be conscience.

There are a number of ways to approach this subject. We will get more specific in subsequent chapters, but for now I have chosen to view the transformational process through the window of one verse. It gives us a clear view into Paul's thinking and provides us with a summary of transformation: "I have been crucified with Christ and *I* no longer live, but Christ lives in *me*. The life *I* live in the body, *I* live by faith in the Son of God, who loved *me* and gave himself for *me*" (Gal. 2:20, emphasis added).

2. For a thorough study see Franz Delitzsch, *A System of Biblical Psychology* (1899; reprint, Grand Rapids: Baker, 1977). The entire book is excellent, particularly see Martin Luther's "Trichotomy" in the appendix to part V, page 460. Another good resource is Wayne Grudem, *Systematic Theology* (Grand Rapids: Zondervan, 1994), 472–89.

You will notice that the personal pronouns *I* and *me* are promi-nent. In the first and second uses of *I* in the verse, Paul said that the "old man" has been crucified. The rest of the verse refers to the "new man" that Paul introduced in 2 Corinthians 5:17, "If anyone is in Christ, he is a new creation; the old has passed away, behold, the new has come" (RSV). In Romans 7:14–25, this "new man" is the regenerate person who desires to please God and is regularly conflicted inside with the spiritual battle (see also Gal. 5:16–17). We experience the new or reborn person inside us as a desire to please God. It is this new person that he describes in the second half of Galatians 2:20 who will also be transformed and morphed into the image of Christ (Rom. 12:2; Gal. 4:19). With that in mind we now consider Paul's first statement.

I HAVE BEEN CRUCIFIED WITH CHRIST

The passive voice indicates that this is something that happened to Paul through a force outside of himself that he couldn't control. Philippians 2:13 states, "For it is God who works in you to will and to act according to his good purpose." It actually goes to the mystery Paul described in Romans that all disciples were once "in Adam" and now are "in Christ" (see Rom. 5:12–21).[3]

It doesn't seem fair that we are held responsible for what the first man did thousands of years ago. But the reality is that we are like Adam and are dominated by sin before Christ enters our lives. It isn't fair either that now we are "in Christ" and therefore have all the benefits of eternal life even though we don't deserve them. The first inequity we disdain, the second we relish. We embrace the truth that in a mysterious and unexplainable way we were there when Adam sinned and we were there when Jesus was crucified. The point is that the new self comes with a new intention and

---

3. This is sometimes called *Federal Headship*; our relationship to Adam was legally established by God and so we were dead in our sin, but now we are in union with Christ through faith, and therefore are released from the penalty of sin.

a new supernatural capacity. Therefore, the new capacity makes transformation possible.

The Interplay of the Body and the Immaterial Nature

Paul pointed out the obvious: "The life I live in the body . . ." (Gal. 2:20). The immaterial nature resides inside a limited container, and the two are so connected that they must be thought of as a team. The fact that we have a body that is limited and sinful doesn't mean that it is bad. The body directed by the immaterial nature can be an awesome tool to advance the kingdom. Case in point: Jesus on the cross. The more serious suffering of becoming sin for us cannot be separated from the physical pain he experienced. We meditate on the beatings, the crown of thorns, the unimaginable suffering involved in crucifixion—the pain in Jesus' body counted for something. The wounds on his wrists, hands, and feet were part of his sacrifice.

This is why the spiritual disciplines have a great deal to do with the body. Such disciplines as fasting, silence, solitude, and stewardship of the body are a way to attack our addictions to stuff, noise, and never being alone. "I have been crucified with Christ" means I live with the intention of heart that I can be free from any habit that enslaves me and that I can acquire any habit that liberates me. That possibility exists because of the entrance of new supernatural powers in Christ.

Subjecting the Will

There is nothing more fundamental to transformation than the taming of the will. The will is wild and unpredictable; it is dripping with lustful thoughts of self-promotion. We live in a culture that worships the ground on which successful people walk. It doesn't make a lot of difference to the general public if you are the greatest painter alive or the greatest skateboarder—you are a celebrity. The brave innovators are lionized; they are interviewed on television, and their books sell. We are told to follow our dreams, don't let anyone stop us, and some day we, too, can become celebrities.

Following Jesus, however, requires a different value system. He is to lead and I am to follow, which means I give up the right to run my own life. Jesus teaches that the greatest among us will be the servant of all, and that might mean laying aside my dream.

At times it has been confusing for me to work out following Jesus. Should I resist the high energy push in me to lead? Should I ignore all my ideas? How aggressive should I be about projects and trips? What is the balance between taking the initiative and making sure I don't get ahead of God's plan?

The only answer I have is to lay my will on the altar and ask God to point the way through fruitfulness. But even the idea that God always calls us to the fruitful and fun is not supported by Scripture. Jesus had periods of great fruitfulness, but he also failed in some situations to get through to people.[4] Our goal is to be transformed into the likeness of Jesus. Our guide is to examine his life and follow the principles of submission and obedience he modeled for us. The personal challenge for me is that it is very often counterintuitive.

I have lived two lives: one as a pastor, the other as writer/spokesman for the disciple-making movement. There are many opportunities that come my way because of my writing and experience in the wider church. At the same time I was a pastor and had obligations to the congregation I served. I have had some scheduling conflicts. There were important matters to deal with at home, but there were crucial tasks to be addressed abroad. Frankly, the opportunities abroad were more fun and seemed to have more impact than some of my pastoral duties. So what would you rather do, preach to 120 leaders who represent six African nations or work

---

4. Jesus was limited in his own hometown (Luke 4:14–30). After healing the demoniac he was asked to leave town (Mark 5:1–17). He seemed to have lost many disciples when things got difficult (John 6:60–66), and he certainly didn't reach the religious establishment (Luke 23–25). Of course it is obvious that Jesus won the ultimate victory, and that is the same promise we have: Serve and follow the will of Jesus as he did the Father and the results will be the right ones.

out a values war between the trustee board and the staff? Would you prefer a nationwide tour to share your vision with eager pastors or the job of massaging differences of opinion on who should be the next worship director? I think you know the answer. But I had to ask what Jesus would do and submit my will to his.

Often God speaks to me through those he has placed over me. Some of my fellow elders think I should slow down and take care of business at home. One of the hardest things I have had to do is cancel some ministry plans that I really wanted to do. That is how Christ is formed in us, when we are willing to give up our personal desires in order to follow him. I will miss the celebrity that comes with those events I cancelled, but isn't that what Jesus meant when he said that if you want to be great, you must be a servant (Matt. 20:26)? The hardest thing about it is that I have to give up control of opportunities that from my perspective are the key to a great future and ministry success.

When I talk about the need for depth, this is one example of what I mean. It is the spiritual strength to surrender our wills to the leadership of Christ even when it means our understanding and desires must be sacrificed. This is a characteristic of servanthood that allows God to use us more powerfully and have a higher impact on those around us in the church. They are moved and inspired by such humility in service, and it knocks down resistance that no great sermon or program can.

The Second Crucifixion

God did what we wouldn't and couldn't; we were mystically in him in the crucifixion. We embrace that through no act of our own we were buried with Christ in baptism into death and were raised with him to newness of life (Rom. 6:1–10). We celebrate that it happened to us in Christ. But there is a second crucifixion in which we do take an active part. That second crucifixion is where we are to be aggressive and ruthless toward the transformation of our character. "Those who belong to Christ Jesus have crucified the sinful nature with its passions and desires" (Gal. 5:24).

Two kinds of crucifixion, two kinds of change: the first is Christ as Savior, the second is Christ as Lord; the first baptized into Christ, the second teaching them to obey everything Christ commanded. They are different but linked; you really can't have one without the other. The idea that we can trust Christ and not intend to obey him is an illusion generated by an unbelieving Christian culture. The belief that we can trust Christ for salvation and that following him is optional is a scourge. It is like saying you trust the pilots who are about to fly your plane but refusing to get on the flight.

Gandhi said if Christians would live according to their beliefs, all people would become Christians. The indictment is that we are living according to our beliefs, and what it proves is that we don't believe Jesus. Case in point is the Sermon on the Mount. We have done some fancy hermeneutical footwork to push its teaching into the future after Jesus returns. Therefore, we have diminished our calling and impact. We claim we must wait until conditions improve as an excuse for not being different and powerful now. The sad result is lives full of religious activity without transformation. We have been reduced to sin management and mediocrity.

So how do we aggressively crucify the sinful nature with its passions and desires? First we must consider the first crucifixion, the new birth, and the second crucifixion, discipleship.

I No Longer Live

Once again we must reidentify *I* as the regenerate believer. This is the same person who in Romans 7:14–25 wanted to please God. The person of the first crucifixion has entered into the second by a natural and full commitment to follow Jesus in discipleship. The starting line is the disciple saying, "I am now a servant, and self-denial is the foundation upon which the formation of Christ's character will rest. And to that end I am committed to take up my cross daily and, as Paul indicated, to die daily."[5]

5. Jesus called us to take up our cross daily. Paul indicated that he was required to die daily to his own flesh and desires (1 Cor. 15:31).

It Starts with Vision

If I have a clear vision of what I want to be like, then I will organize my life around what Jesus taught and did. I will consider myself dead to sin and offer my earthly instrument as a means to display his life (Rom. 6:2, 11, 13). And I will begin practicing the spiritual disciplines.

Learning to live in the disciplines that lead to real transformation is similar to learning a foreign language. My wife, Jane, has always been bold and adventurous. She grew up in a small resort town next to a large lake. It was the kind of resort that the villain Jason in the Halloween films would have liked, kind of a "Red Neck" Riviera. Needless to say, her school's foreign language program was understaffed, consisting only of Mrs. Jones, who taught Latin. But Jane wanted to be an airline attendant, fly with TWA, and live in Paris, France, so she needed to know French. But in 1963 the only thing French in Grove, Oklahoma, were fries and salad dressing. Armed with nothing more than some vision, Jane and a friend successfully petitioned the school for a French class. She studied hard for a couple of years, and although she never became an airline attendant or lived in Paris, today Jane remembers enough to order dinner in a French restaurant.

A lack of strong sustaining vision explains why most high school foreign language classes in the U.S. don't work. They may be required classes, but unless the students have the vision to really learn another language, there is usually very little benefit. On the other hand, I am amazed by how many people are learning English around the world. Jane and I were having dinner in Romania and were impressed with our waiter's English. He couldn't have been more than eighteen, so I asked him if he studied English in school. "No, I learned it watching TV." What drove the young man was an intense desire to live in America. People are learning English around the world in order to improve their lives. They willingly submit themselves to discipline so they can reach their goal.

If you really want to learn another language, you will discipline yourself to study the language, attempt to live among people who speak that language, and learn the nuances of the language and culture until it becomes part of you and you actually begin to think in that language. If our vision of becoming like Christ is compelling, we can submit to the spiritual disciplines necessary long enough for them to become a natural part of our lives and to see change as a result.

The Value of a Society

People committed to personal transformation need each other. It is imperative that when we decide to follow Jesus, to choose the life he led, we must join with others with the same vision, intention, and submissive spirit. The more we immerse ourselves in the discipleship culture with kindred spirits, the more quickly we will become part of the new culture. So we will begin to think, pray, feel, and desire the same things as Jesus. Not perfectly, but there will be a transformation of viewpoint and intention.

Recently I learned of a man in our faith community who wanted to follow Jesus with regard to possessions. He was convicted that he should tithe to the church, but he couldn't because of the large mortgage payment on his big house. He sold his house and reduced his debt so he could begin to tithe. That is transformation; that is the kind of change that inspires Christians and seekers alike. I was so impressed that it created in me a desire to be a more careful steward. This kind of transformation is contagious; it inspires others to examine their lives and deepens the desire to please God.

I encourage ministries to form Choose the Life communities in which those attempting to change from laissez-faire, nonaccountable Christianity to following Jesus can help one another. Like a group of immigrants landing on foreign soil, we learn to speak the language and create the discipleship culture together. What other choice do we have? To continue to languish in churches that are not challenging their people and that are not penetrating their culture is unacceptable.

CHRIST LIVES IN ME

Now that Paul's proposition, "I no longer live" (Gal. 2:20), has me out of the way, how does Christ move in? The illustration that helps me is the Israelites being promised the land. God gave them the land, but they had to go in and conquer it. So it is with our spirits. God gives us the power to overcome the flesh, but the flesh and the Spirit "are opposed to each other, to prevent [us] from doing what [we] would do" (Gal. 5:17 RSV). God's power gives us strength to overcome the desires of the flesh and follow Christ, but we must be watchful all our earthly days.

The battle for control of my inner person is illustrated by my day at the 2002 Christian Booksellers Association convention in Anaheim, California. I went with great expectations because my new book, *Straight Talk on Spiritual Power,* was being released. Yes, the convention was glitzy; yes, there was tons of Jesus junk and holy hardware; and yes, some of it was tacky. Publishers went all out, and some of the displays were remarkable. As I wound my way through the labyrinth of displays, I encountered long lines of people waiting at celebrity booths where well-known writers were signing books. I made my way past John MacArthur and Kathy Ireland.

Finally I arrived at my publisher's booth. I scanned the large placards that displayed the new books. I saw everything from new books on diet and exercise to how to cook like a Christian, but no placard for me. I took a deep breath and thanked the Lord, by faith, and began to look for a copy of my new book amid the fifty or more new releases. It wasn't there. With a bit of irritation rising up within, I approached a salesman. But before I could ask him the whereabouts of my new book, he brushed past me saying, "Excuse me, sir, I need something out of this drawer." Not one of the salesmen knew me or anything about my new book.

I left with a smile on my face thinking, "That is really funny, Lord. You really let me have it there, didn't you? If you died for me, at least I can be humiliated at CBA for you."

Just then I turned the corner and walked into the largest and most elaborate publisher's booth. It was two stories, with a hospitality lounge on the second level. At the top of the stairs was the author whose book on Jabez had sold six million copies. I have worked hard on the nine books I have written, and they are all good. But the total royalties from all nine of my books are a drop in a bucket compared to royalties on six million sales. At that moment if my flesh could have had its way, I would have fallen to my knees in front of the two-story testament to America's "it's all about me" spirituality and cried, "Why not me?" Which demonstrated that at that moment, it was all about me.[6]

So when I speak of winning the inner struggle with my flesh, it is still in theory that I no longer live, but Christ now lives in me. But can it be more than a theory? Can we really change? There are some who just give up and accept mediocrity at this point; manage our sin but not put away our sin, wanting to be transformed just to the point that we don't sin as much. Too many of us are fatalistic: "I can't stop smoking, overeating, holding grudges, being afraid to speak about my faith. That's just not me!" Indeed, it's not me or you, but Christ can gain much ground in our souls, and we can begin to take on his character. It is more than asking, What would Jesus do? It is, What did Jesus teach? What did Jesus feel? What did Jesus believe?

The Inner Workings in Action

Thus far our focused view through the window of Galatians 2:20 has explained the inner workings of transformation in theological terms mixed with mystery. Concepts such as crucifixion with Christ, I no longer live, and Christ now lives through me are embraceable but are not enough to motivate. The theology and mystery is tempered, however, with the simple phrase, "The life I live in the body, I live by faith in the Son of God, who loved me and gave himself for me" (Gal. 2:20).

6. I read *The Prayer of Jabez* and even have a *Prayer of Jabez* rock in my office. I really have enjoyed Bruce Wilkinson's ministry and particularly liked *Secrets of the Vine* and *The Life that God Rewards*. My apologies to Bruce for dragging him into my own sin problems.

The body is a tool for God; Christ himself lives inside, and his transformation of us is triggered by faith. Because he loved us, we respond in willing submission to his leadership. Remember, we have defined *faith* as action based on confident belief. Jesus defined *faith* as following him, and when we do that, the reshaping kicks in supernaturally.[7] When our desire is to think and act like Jesus, then the natural circumstances of life provide the opportunity to grow. This is when Jesus' life in us gains ground.

One of our first tests as a married couple was in 1969, when Jane and I were applying for seminary. I had not been accepted, but rather than wait for word from the school, we moved by faith to Wilmore, Kentucky, the home of Asbury Theological Seminary. We rented a very nice upstairs apartment near campus. It had hardwood floors, and the morning sun filled the room with its brightness and warmth.

The day we were to move in, the young couple who were already living there had a change of plans and asked to stay. Since we had already signed a rental agreement and paid our rent, we had the right to move in. The landlord asked us what we wanted to do—move into the upstairs rooms we loved so much or into the dark, dank basement apartment with tiny little slits that masqueraded as windows. The basement apartment had brown tile floors, block walls, and plenty of varmints that loved the moist lower regions of the building.

We sat down on the steps and prayed, asking the simple question, What did Jesus model and teach about this situation? He had said that if someone asks for your shirt, give him your coat as well. He modeled putting others first before your own needs. After our prayer and discussion, it was the easiest thing in the world to take the basement. We did so and never regretted or looked back in a negative way. In fact, it was a pleasure to do it because we felt so blessed to be able to live like our Lord in a very small way.

This seminal decision set into place a pattern for the remainder of our lives. It was like laying the first stone in a pathway to follow-

---

7. Luke 9:23–25 says that faith is following Jesus and submitting to him as Leader. The reshaping or morphing is taught in Romans 8:29; 12:2; and Galatians 4:19.

ing Jesus. Over the last thirty-four years we have laid many more stepping-stones. As we look back we can see how God blessed and/or used every step. It just so happened that a few weeks later we left Wilmore to join Athletes in Action. We didn't need that apartment anyway, and God knew it.

What actually happened in that case regarding the inner working of transformation? The desire to follow Jesus overpowered the desire to have something better. This gets back to the question, What is the good life? Jesus defined the good life as living for others, not worrying about material needs now, in fact sending them ahead to heaven for safekeeping by using them now for his kingdom (see Matt. 5–7, the Sermon on the Mount). It doesn't go back to our superior knowledge of Scripture or an extra dose of goodness. The decision to give up the better apartment goes to the definition of *better*. The better apartment was in the basement, because the blessing was in the basement. There are eternal rewards that are so delicious and attractive that they can't be resisted. There is a depth of joy that can be experienced right now that once you have tasted, you want more and more. It went back more to a fundamental decision Jane and I had made to choose a certain kind of life, to follow Jesus' life and example and make our decisions based on what he would do.

So it could be said that the inner workings of transformation are based on vision planted in the heart of every believer to be like Christ. Then through an act of faith we follow, take up our cross daily, deny our flesh what opposes and distracts, and choose his way.

Inside Out or Outside In?

Maybe you have heard actors talk about their craft. Most of them have a philosophy of character development as inside out or outside in. Some begin inside with how the script describes the character and then build an internal emotional structure that is the basis for the character's speech and action in the text. Others start on the outside with the character's clothes, voice, facial expressions, even special makeup with prosthetics. For example, in *Rainman* Dustin Hoffman worked inside out, while in *Tootsie* he worked outside in.

Actors use both methods to get into character. Isn't it much the same with followers of Jesus? God works both inside out and outside in. God works inside out through prayer, Bible reading, and the practice of the spiritual disciplines. I resist the constructs that posture transformation as only an internal activity because there is also an external dimension. God also works outside in when we serve or fit into a prescribed external regime such as church worship, service projects, and even the wearing of special clothes (i.e., clerical robes, choir robes, monks' or nuns' attire, and religious school uniforms that all have religious significance). One of the most dramatic changes we witness is people returning from short-term mission experiences. Their worldview and values are radically changed by simple acts of obedience outside the spiritual disciplines or any process.

GOD'S TRANSFORMATIONAL COMBINATIONS

Character is shaped in community.[8] God uses Scripture, relationships, and circumstances in a powerful combination to reshape our wills. So while the flesh never improves, God actually works in our lives to shape our will as it submits to his purpose (Phil. 2:13). What I desire today is very different from what I desired even five years ago. God has changed my will; it is not tamed, but it is transformed. How did it happen? Future chapters will get more specific, but an example here is needed.

Recently we asked congregational focus groups what event or experience had caused the most important spiritual transformation in the last year. There were two themes: trauma and accountable relationships. Proactive training is sterile without the bacteria of trauma and relationships. Intentional training is essential, and we

8. Bill Thrall and Bruce McNicol, *Forming the High-Trust Culture* (Leadership Catalyst, 2000), A-1, A-6.

can always count on trauma to show up. Then relationships in community both challenge us and support us. Anyone who thinks transformation is only the contemplative life is naïve, and life will seem very rude to them.

God's gift to me the past five years has been to break my will and then rebuild it. The first thing he used was my desire to build an already good church into a great one. After ten years of teaching and training pastors, I naturally started out with a really good strategic plan. I laid out a five-year plan with specific goals and made decisions based on my vast global experience. The plan rolled off the congregation's back like the proverbial water off the duck. Everyone agreed with me, nodded their heads, and didn't respond. We had permission and agreement but not ownership. People misread my plan as self-promoting and personal kingdom building rather than beneficial to them as individuals. No matter how well I preached or communicated, regardless of innovation, fundamentally there was no behavior change.

This created a growing sense of frustration in me and a myriad of adjustments, restarts, and new innovations upon new innovations. It was like trying to corral cats; there was a great deal of independence among the people and no compelling reason to change. I kept giving off the odor of self-promotion. I did not sense it in my heart and don't believe it was there that strongly. But after ten years on the road, I was ministering out of my conceptual portfolio rather than connecting deeply at an emotional level.

Because the vision had not broken through the wall of resistance, the plan was not working. This led to a growing perception that I was a CEO type pastor—my way or the highway. People started to abandon ship, slipping off in their little lifeboats a few at a time. There was a directional malaise that set in; we were not feeling well, but we were not sure why. All my competence wasn't working; my ideas and strategies were failing. This is when I wanted to run, but God clearly told me, "I'm going to break you. Don't run."

God encouraged me through words of prophecy that he would bless our church. But some of those words also said I would be going through the fire. God used the circumstances of my ideas not working in combination with the personal pain. He gave me enough encouragement to stay, but he humbled me. He showed me my pride and arrogance and how futile all my efforts had been. Because God won't bless the proud, only the humble get his best (1 Peter 5:5–10). He showed me that I was thinking and operating out of my head when I needed to be much more in my heart.

God showed me that if I were to love as Christ loved, I would have to do it in a way that the members of my church could understand as love. That meant I would have to submit myself to more process and listen to those around me. I hate to sit and process ideas and then compose some sort of relationally based missional stew. But God showed me that the way others could experience my love was to give them the gift of my participation in the planning process. So my new commitment was to find a way to love them so they really understood that I loved them. My will was now being reshaped. What I wanted more than numerical success was the nod from others that they were experiencing my love. And God really put my new desire to the test.

A very strong leader in our church led a mini-rebellion to challenge my design for small groups. We were able to meet together and eventually find common ground, but in the process there had been some confusion and hurt feelings. Stories circulated that led some families to leave the church. This was a major setback for the church in finances, morale, and in how people perceived me, their pastor. It seemed the more humble I became before God and others, the worse things became.

A few weeks later I got word that the leader in question claimed that God wasn't working at our church anymore. I was furious. The gall, the hubris, and the arrogance of such a statement. Then it hit me; I was just as arrogant as the leader but in a different way. I was angry not only about what was said but because it called into question my integrity and reputation. My old will wanted vindication; my reshaped will asked how I could show love to this person. My reshaped will, crafted by the pain of community, won out. There was an inward change in attitude expressed in the new words I spoke and the actions I took. It was based on my faith rooted in

God's love and his gift for me. He loved me and gave himself for me, and I knew I could safely give myself back to him by trusting his way over mine. And after a while his way became my way.

FEAR

Another issue that I have had to deal with is fear. The most common exhortation in Scripture is not to be holy, be good, or don't sin. It is simply, "Don't be afraid." A total of 366 times we are told not to fear. Being able to obey one of these 366 commands requires a reshaping of our souls, because faith is only real in obedience.

Fear seems to be in the air; we eat, sleep, and breathe fear. We are afraid of being alone, being unloved, or being abandoned. When we are young we are afraid of being stupid or of not fitting in with our peers. When we enter the workforce we are afraid we might not get the right job or that we can't perform once we get it. Many more today are afraid of marriage or fear they cannot be good parents. We look ahead to retirement and worry if we will have enough money. We fear growing older, not being able to take care of ourselves, dying suddenly.

There is much to fear, and Paul struggled with it like many of us. He also gave us the reason we should not fear. The Corinthian church had rebelled against his leadership, and he was responding in his most emotional letter, called Second Corinthians:

> For we do not want you to be ignorant, brethren, of the affliction we experienced in Asia; for we were so utterly, unbearably crushed that we despaired of life itself. Why, we felt that we had received the sentence of death; but that was to make us rely not on ourselves but on God who raises the dead.
>
> 2 Corinthians 1:8–9 RSV

Paul was saying something quite radical when he stated that all the fears were for one reason, "to make us rely not on ourselves but on God who raises the dead." Believing in the resurrection means we don't need to be afraid. Any God who can raise the dead can be trusted with our fear of loneliness or rejection, with our homes, children, jobs, marriages, health care, money, and old age. And yes, a God who raises the dead can be trusted with my death. God wants us to stop fearing and follow him. But as N. T. Wright says, the point is, "Until you learn to live without fear you won't find it easy to follow Jesus."[9]

The travel required for my ministry means I often need to make choices that could put me in harm's way. The threats of terrorism, fear of disease outbreaks, and other elements of travel in unfriendly parts of the world are matters of concern. It helps me to read Paul's catalog of catastrophes: the beatings, shipwrecks, hours floating in the sea, extended time in jail, and all the dangers of travel in the first century from robbers (2 Cor. 11:23–29). Yet Paul continued traveling and relying on "God who raises the dead."

As I wonder if I should go, the words that strike me most are "fear not." If I shrink back from opportunities that God puts before me because of fear, I am going to have trouble following Jesus where he leads me. How about you? Much like Teresa of Avila's interior castle analogy, Jesus draws me further and further in, toward the center room of his presence.[10] The less I fear, the easier it will be for me to follow him.

9. N. T. Wright, *Following Jesus: Biblical Reflections on Discipleship* (Grand Rapids: Eerdmans, 1994), 67.

10. Teresa of Avila, *The Interior Castle* (New York: Paulist Press, 1979). This is based on a vision she had on Trinity Sunday, 1577. She saw a castle made entirely out of a diamond or of a very clear crystal in which there were many rooms, just as in heaven there are many dwelling places. Each room moves us closer to the center where the King of Glory dwells in the greatest splendor.

6

THE MIND
AND THE LIFE

Coming to grips with the post-Christian mind will
not exercise the brain in the way it was exercised in
defining the Christian mind. For there is no fixed
body of opinion, no homogeneous set of principles,
no philosophical rationale informing that amorphous
accumulation of half-truths on which the popular
mind is fed by the media today. . . . It would be a mistake to look for a system or coherence. . . . It would be
like looking for signposts in the jungle. . . . The distinction between the Christian mind and the post-
Christian mind is the difference between civilization
and the jungle.[1]

—Harry Blamires

1. Harry Blamires, *The Post-Christian Mind* (Ann Arbor, Mich.: Servant Publications,
1999), 11.

There is no doubt that the need for transformed minds has never been greater. There was a time when most of society held a fixed body of opinion to be true. There was a solid moral base for right and wrong. You could sit down with a Jew, a Muslim, a Christian, a Mormon, even an agnostic, and find basic moral agreement. The philosophical jungle Blamires speaks of is where we now reside. There has been a multiplication in ports of origin from which people start the journey to truth, but the desired destination has not changed, that being the mind of Christ (1 Cor. 2:16).

THE MIND OF CHRIST

Personal transformation begins with the acquisition of the mind of Christ. Our minds are wired in such a way that we have thoughts that create images, feelings, and perceptions. Even spontaneous, unconscious action is based on a cognitive memory that is fixed in the mind. (Which explains why every time I think of eating liver, I immediately gag.) This is why Paul taught that transformation begins by the reprogramming of the mind (Rom. 12:2). Just as every human's actions are based on what he or she thinks, one cannot conceive being like Christ without thinking like Christ.

To have the mind of Christ is both necessary and expected, but the contemporary mind is far from it. Some believe freethinking is a mind not tied down by absolutist restraints. Historically, free-thinking has been associated with liberalism and drugs. Liberals claimed there was no final truth, and some claimed that drugs would expand the mind.

Aldous Huxley, a British intellectual and author of *Brave New World*, was the darling of the Bohemian leftist literary elite in Europe and later in the United States. He was one of the first to experiment with LSD in the 1950s, and he coined the word *psychedelic*. The famous or infamous rock band "The Doors" paid homage to Huxley by taking their name from his book *Doors of Perception*. It is amazing just how much influence Huxley had on those who preferred any kind of mind-expanding experience over submission to the absolutes offered in Scripture.

Many of Huxley's followers combined politics and drugs, and the results were Woodstock and the Weathermen.[2] There were also other professors, writers, and leaders who convinced the next generation that truth as a category had collapsed. The result is a generation of younger Americans who have lost the ability to think properly about truth. They are lost, wandering in Blamires's jungle, desiring truth, but only searching for their own personal truth—tiny truth, only true enough for themselves and no one else. It is a far cry from what Francis Schaeffer called "True Truth"—a truth for everyone that is found only in the mind of Christ.

WE ARE CALLED TO A NEW MIND

The renewing of the mind is nothing less than the total interchange of our ideas, perceptions, images, and feelings for those of Christ. That is why we must *choose* the life; we won't simply drift into transformation of the mind. There will be no Star Trek mind melds or palm pilot information dumps with Jesus' wisdom

2. For our younger readers, Woodstock was a rock concert in 1968 at which 400,000 people gathered near Woodstock, New York. It was for many the apex for freedom of expression, sex, drugs, and rock and roll. The Weathermen was a violent terrorist organization that challenged the authority of government and what they called the evils of capitalist society. Most of them are now in their late fifties, are worried about their stock portfolios, and are planning on retiring to the good life.

dancing on laser beams. It will require a disciplined focus and a change in the way we exercise our minds. Another way to think of it is that it is a change in frame of mind. "Let this mind be in you which was also in Christ Jesus" (Phil. 2:5 NKJV).[3]

We know that the mind can be trained. Paul taught that we can rid ourselves of anxiety by following a disciplined procedure mixed with prayer (Phil. 4:6–9). The alternative to worry is prayer—releasing the load of angst to God and imagining that Christ himself will march guard duty around our minds. Paul then encouraged the readers to reprogram their minds: "Whatever is true, whatever is noble, whatever is right, whatever is pure, whatever is lovely, whatever is admirable—if anything is excellent or praiseworthy—*think about such things*" (Phil. 4:8, emphasis added).

Paul believed that a person could change from an anxiety-ridden, double-minded person to a positive thinker. How many people do you know who have made a change that great? I have spent my entire adult life working with Christians, and I know a few who have changed to that extent. But sadly, most gave up on changing their thought patterns. The general Christian populace will not be transformed without a conscious decision to choose the spiritual disciplines, the life of discipleship. Without transformation, there is little chance of raising the level of power of life and testimony. Thus, the ineptness continues, the worried Christian blends in with the worried secularist, and they walk together into an uncertain future.

Paul didn't give up that easily, though, and neither should we. He spoke of his own struggles and victories: "Whatever you have learned or received or heard from me, or seen in me—*put it into practice*. And the God of peace will be with you" (Phil. 4:9, emphasis added). Before we can put these things into practice, we must think about them. But not for hours, days, months, or years—only for seconds. As we grow in Christ this process will become more automatic as we begin to think differently and then

3. The word *phronos* in this text refers to a frame of mind or attitude. It assumes a certain mind-set. This is distinct from the more simple word for mind, *nous*.

experience events differently. Paul testified that he "learned to be content" regardless of his outward conditions, which led him to, "I can do everything through him who gives me strength" (Phil. 4:11, 13).

STRONGHOLDS

In order for our minds to be transformed, we must overcome the strongholds that currently control our thoughts and actions. There are a number of ways to describe strongholds. Some say they are demons to be exorcised; others describe them as thought patterns to be changed. The Scriptures explain, "For though we live in the world, we do not wage war as the world does. The weapons we fight with are not the weapons of the world. On the contrary, they have divine power to demolish strongholds" (2 Cor. 10:3–4). I take this to mean that we don't fight solely with the intellect; this is more basic than a war of words or a debate environment. Strongholds are arguments or pretensions that posture themselves as alternatives to the truth of God. Satan builds the strongholds through his very effective programming of the postmodern mind. But God's power can destroy the strongholds by exposing the falsehood of long-held beliefs.

One of the most common false ideologies is that "people don't change." This is folklore more than philosophy, and I heard it first on the front porch from Uncle Gibb as he alternated between talking and lobbing the remnants of his tobacco chaw into the spittoon. Uncle Gibb said Cousin Paul was no good and never would be any good. He was an alcoholic who couldn't keep a job but was really good at "breeding." The evidence of both was his six kids living in poverty on a nearby farm.

At least Uncle Gibb believed that Cousin Paul was morally responsible for who he was. The cynical argument that people can't change has moved from the realm of folklore and entered the fast-developing world of genetics, where scientists furiously seek the fat gene, the anger gene, the promiscuity gene. We have gone from believing people can't change because of a "bad seed" to believing we can't change because of our genetic makeup, and so we are not responsible for our actions.

I do believe we are hardwired with a temperament and a basic personality. Every parent knows this to be true, especially if they have more than one child. The differences in people's temperaments and personalities are illustrated nearly every day through everything from what we eat to how we handle adversity. But I also believe that our personalities and bents can be shaped to reflect kindness instead of harshness, forgiveness rather than grudge holding, submission in place of rebellion.

MY STRONGHOLD

I believed a false idea for many years. I was convinced that there was 25 percent of the population for whom I had no responsibility because there was no way they would respond to me. Like many of you, I had taken the battery of personality inventories that are so popular in our culture. I recall one in particular that called me a "Driver" personality, and there was another personality that didn't trust Drivers and would always question the Driver's motives and integrity. I was sure that every local church had at least 25 percent of that personality type and that I would collide with them on a regular basis.

Over the years when someone would disagree with my teaching or say they didn't know where I was coming from, I would simply say to myself, "That's a 25 percenter. They will be out the door soon." I would just write it off as the cost of doing business, resting in my false belief that there really wasn't anything I could do about it.

Then one day God demolished that stronghold by revealing to me what it meant to love as Christ loved. Jesus commanded us to love one another as he has loved us. Of course I knew about that, but an overwhelming truth came over me that the only reason I was following Jesus was that I was convinced he loves me. He had gotten through to me by loving me in such a way that I truly experienced his love. He didn't hold anything back; he offered himself up for me. Then I thought of those people who didn't think I loved or cared for them. Immediately I knew the application: I must make a commitment to find a way to love them so they would experience my love in a way they understood.

That decision liberated me from a stronghold that had been hurting my teaching and work. In some cases I have broken through by listening, by submitting myself to elongated decision-making procedures, and by rewarding feedback on a variety of issues. These adjustments have been very hard for me because I am energized by ideas, and when I see the goal, I want to launch right into the project. The majority of people, however, need to be given time to process through a series of exposures in order to accept change. So my gift of love has been to submit to that process. As the African proverb tells us, "If you want to go fast, go alone. If you want to go far, go together."

Strongholds die hard, which is why they must be demolished by more than argument. It takes insight and conviction of the Holy Spirit to loosen the tight grip they have on us.

WHAT IS IN OUR MINDS

My mind is packed with a conglomerate of thoughts and feelings, much of it subconscious, that inform and sometimes control my ability to submit my will to God. There are many ways to go about putting labels on what happens inside those little gray cells. I have chosen three:

Ideas: beliefs based on life experience and worldview
Images: concrete and specific pictures or memories of life
Feelings: passions and desires that we experience[4]

4. This helpful construct of ideas, images, and feelings comes from Dallas Willard, *Renovation of the Heart* (Colorado Springs: NavPress, 2003), 95–140. I want to acknowledge Willard's influence here, but I take full credit or blame for the content.

There are years of experience packed in our minds—everything from how to spell *cat* to the sensation we felt at our first kiss. Those experiences create vivid images and feelings such as my memory of how I felt as a toddler watching elementary students walking to school as they passed my yard. I remember them smiling and waving to me as I peered at them between the bars of my playpen. Not all memories are so pleasant. I have intense feelings of regret for not being able to meet my father, along with the rejection I experienced when he refused to see me after I had contacted him a few years before his death.

Some memories or emotions may be sitting on the bottom of your mind waiting, and it may take you by surprise when they are triggered and suddenly come to the surface. I planned to speak at my grandfather's funeral, and I had it all together until I opened my mouth and nothing came out. Something so deep I didn't know it was there rushed up my throat, and I was paralyzed. All I could do was return to my seat.

Transformation through the renewing of the mind can be a wrenching experience. It can require finding a new perspective on images and feelings fixed firmly in our memory or abandoning long-held beliefs and attitudes. As an example of an incorrect, long-held belief, some people may think they have a tremendous talent when they don't. Jane and I were invited to a dinner/concert at a new parishioner's home. The couple were so kind, and the meal was sumptuous. But then came the concert. We sat down in the wife's recording room where she practiced her craft. Her husband said she had given up a lucrative career in show business to use her singing voice for the Lord. We were now going to be blessed by her vocal gift, and of course she would sing in church pro bono. The background tape began, and I bit my lip as I heard the opening notes to "Feelings," a seventies hit that has been ridiculed ever since as the consummate lounge song. Our hostess flipped back her hair, took a sultry pose, and then hit a note that is not written on any sheet music. The concert continued downhill from there.

Suffice it to say that I felt like the critic who described Margaret Truman's recital as a difficult experience. He wondered if she would reach her goal—the end of the song.[5] What made our hostess's concert almost tragic was that for years her husband had perpetuated the myth that she could sing. He had served as her agent, spending thousands of dollars on equipment and press releases. The fact that she did not have a good voice would someday be a painful truth she would have to accept.

There are many other false beliefs and attitudes that must be transformed. Some people think they are perceptive and they are not. Others advocate their own homespun spirituality when they don't even know Martin Luther from Martin Luther King. There are people who don't believe they have much to offer, but they do. These and many more false beliefs, based on ideas, images, and feelings, can have a strong grip on our actions.

TRANSFORMED IDEAS

Ideas are how we assign meaning to what we see and hear. They are also Satan's primary focus in his effort to thwart God's purpose. Once we are subject to his ideas, he can go to work on someone else because we are defeated.[6]

Beginning with Eve, Satan's primary strategy was to instill the idea that God cannot be trusted. Satan asked Eve, "Did God really say . . . ?" Then he built on that seed of doubt with an accusation, "For God knows that when you eat of it your eyes will be opened, and you will be like God, knowing good and evil" (Gen. 3:5). Satan is the personification of pride and self-sufficiency. He told Eve what he tells every person, what the secular culture screams every day, "God cannot be trusted; take matters into your own hands to secure your future."

The basic message in all temptation is, "Take charge, take what you need, and take it now." The Enemy loves to tempt us with thoughts such as:

5. David McCullough, *Truman* (New York: Simon & Schuster, 1992).
6. See 2 Corinthians 2:11. Satan's strategy is deception in *noema*, or thought and design.

I can't wait till marriage for sex; I've got to have it now.

What if I don't find the right person? I'm getting older; it will all pass me by.

I can't wait for God to lead me to a new job. I'll take anything right now.

God will never change my spouse. I'm unhappy, so I'll find someone new.

It is all about fear that God won't come through. We don't see God working, so we think, "I've got to do something, get something moving, take some action, produce some result."

Fear and a lack of trust are Satan's bread and butter. But remember that there are 366 *fear not*s in Scripture—that's more than one for each day of the year. The antidote for fear and lack of trust is the healing words of Scripture:

> Trust in the LORD with all your heart
> and lean not on your own understanding;
> in all your ways acknowledge him,
> and he will make your paths straight.
>
> Proverbs 3:5–6

Do not let your hearts be troubled. Trust in God; trust also in me [Jesus].

> John 14:1

Whoever follows me [Jesus] will never walk in darkness, but will have the light of life.

> John 8:12

> God is our refuge and strength,
> an ever-present help in trouble.
> Therefore we will not fear.
>
> Psalm 46:1–2

These words soothe the soul, heal scars, and build confidence. Jesus is our Leader, and following him sometimes means waiting on him to put things in order. Waiting on God is not waiting around; it is actively persevering in obedience as we wait for God to orchestrate circumstances.

We have grown accustomed to our own ideas and are in the habit of relying on them. The constant temptation is to grab the proverbial bull by the horns and make things happen. We might say we can't stand one more day, one more hour, or one more minute of waiting. But listen to some more transformational words:

> No temptation has seized you except what is common to man. And God is faithful; he will not let you be tempted beyond what you can bear. But when you are tempted, he will also provide a way out so that you can stand up under it.
>
> 1 Corinthians 10:13

Transformation is about adopting new ideas, such as the truths listed above. Transformation can be realized in bearing up to a temptation or getting away from the temptation. God will not allow you to be smashed by temptation; instead he can be trusted to provide a means to stand up to it.

The strongest temptation of all can be the desire to run our own lives, to take charge now. Finding the balance between being passive and taking action is a constant challenge that won't disappear as long as our minds are flawed and our lust exists. This is why it is so crucial to develop the capacity to hear God's voice. As Henri Nouwen wrote, "I know that I have to move from speaking about Jesus to letting him speak within me, from thinking about Jesus to letting him think within me, from acting for and with Jesus to letting him act through me."[7]

7. Henri Nouwen, quoted in *Seeds of Hope: A Henri Nouwen Reader*, ed. Robert Durback (New York: Image Books, 1989), 5.

Some of Satan's Favorite Ideas

Satan does not want us to have a transformed mind. He enjoys thwarting us with his own ideas and perversions of the truth. Some of his favorites are:

IF GOD IS IN IT, THEN A BLESSED LIFE WILL BE EASY AND FUN AND WILL RUN SMOOTHLY.

Why is the most common prayer in Christendom, "May the event go smoothly"? It joins the chorus of other platitudes: "God's work done in God's way will never lack God's resources." "God's blessing is in evidence in numerical growth, financial stability, and a congregation free of conflict."

Try this stuff out on the church in Rwanda, where 75 percent of the pastors were killed in tribal genocide in 1994 and 15 percent more fled the country. The average income in Rwanda is one hundred U.S. dollars a month. They don't expect it to go smoothly. So why is it that these godly men and women don't have all the resources they need? Don't they read the right books and send money to the right televangelist?

Satan loves it when we allow our culture to set the standards for the church. He wants us to believe in a Christianity built on Western capitalistic social structures. Jesus, however, promised difficulty and persecution, saying that we should be glad because he will turn it into good (Matt. 5:11–13; John 16:33; Rom. 8:28–29; James 1:2–4).

RELIGION IS A PRIVATE MATTER.

When the person seated next to me on the airplane found out I was in the "God business," she said what so many would like to but rarely do, "You're not going to try to convert me, are you?" I pondered what to say, and then it came to me, "I wouldn't be much of a Christian if I didn't try to convert you." I told her that I was held responsible by God to tell others, to witness to my experience with God (Acts 1:8). Since I believed I had the best news anyone could hear, I was going to tell her. As it turned out, she hadn't heard the Good News; she had only been exposed to bits and pieces like so many Americans.

One of Satan's favorite false ideas is that religion is a private matter, because nice and benign Christians are no threat to him. He wants us to worship the God of tolerance and political correctness. I predict that one day in the not-too-distant future witnessing to the exclusive nature of the gospel will be classified as a "hate crime." The thought police will turn in people who speak words that exclude and make people feel left out and guilty. Churches will exhort members to let their lives speak but won't ask them to say anything or take a stand. One of the most arrogant things a person can say is, "I will let my life speak for me." As Sam Shoemaker used to say, "that is too much about us and too little about him." This is another idea that must be taken captive and thrown in jail (2 Cor. 10:5).

SOME THINGS ARE UNFORGIVABLE; OTHER THINGS ARE FORGIVABLE, BUT THE OFFENDER MUST ASK BEFORE YOU FORGIVE.

When the Roman soldiers were gambling over Jesus' clothes and mocking him while he died, not one asked for Jesus' forgiveness. Yet he offered it, "Father, forgive them, for they do not know what they are doing" (Luke 23:34). If there was ever anything unforgivable, it was this gross act of injustice. The only perfect human was being killed, and he was bearing the sins of Adolf Hitler, Joseph Stalin, and every other soul to ever live (2 Cor. 5:21).

Regardless of Jesus' example, Satan's false idea about forgiveness has a strong hold on our culture and continues to destroy families and communities. The entire nation paid attention when Governor George Ryan of Illinois commuted the sentences of every death-row inmate in his state. His actions were applauded by death penalty opponents, but capital punishment advocates were outraged. The real conundrum, however, was for the families of the victims of these inmates. They must live somewhere between justice and forgiveness. Some insist that the crime of murder of their loved one was so heinous that it can never be forgiven.

I don't pretend to understand the emotional roller coaster of pain the victims' families ride, but I know there is a deep release into liberty when we forgive. You may remember when a young Turk shot Pope John Paul II. After he recovered, the Pope visited his assailant and forgave him. The transformed mind believes that any and all offenses against us are forgivable. Anything less is to not understand the depth of our own sin and the mercy of the cross.

BE CAREFUL WHAT YOU PRAY FOR; YOU MIGHT GET IT.

Oscar Wilde, a nineteenth-century playwright of such classics as *The Importance of Being Earnest*, was even better known by some for his sardonic quips concerning the ironies of life. He said that by age forty people have the face they deserve. He endeared himself to many chocolate addicts with "I can resist everything except temptation." Even though he wasn't a man of prayer, he said, "There are two tragedies in life—one is not getting what you want, the other is getting it." This attitude reveals a twisted image of God.

Satan wants to breed fear, doubt, and insecurity in God's children. I have encountered so many fellow followers of Jesus who feel guilt or apprehension about doing well. Recently a friend was lamenting that things were going really well in his life, almost too well. He said, "I am just waiting for the other shoe to fall." He laughed, but he really meant it.

What does it reveal about our view of God that being treated well sends us reeling outside our comfort zone? Satan's goal is to make us live with uncertainty, thinking that our Father is unpredictable. Satan loves it when we fear that one minute our face is cupped lovingly in God's hands and the next the back of his hand strikes us down.

He Likes Me; He Really Likes Me

Most of us struggle with insecurities—even famous celebrities do. Who can forget Sally Fields's honest burst of joy at the receipt of her second Academy Award. Her deep sense of wonder exploded, "You like me; you really like me." I think she was truly blessed and surprised that such a competitive, jealous, and often ruthless bunch as her fellow actors really thought her work was worthy of such honor.

Not long ago I made a decision to follow my heart, to take a risk, to try a new way in the quest to return the church to its disciple-making roots. God had been stirring in me for over a year to make the change. The decision was agony; it meant leaving behind the church I so deeply loved. It meant walking away from a predictable income stream, and at age fifty-six it seemed too risky. But all arrows pointed in that direction—it was a for-this-I-was-born moment. When people asked me what I would do, I shrugged my shoulders and quipped, "I follow a cloud by day and pillar of fire at night." I wrestled with what God really thought of all this. Was this my flesh rearing its ugly head? I really didn't know.

I told the elders on a Thursday night of my decision, and they were very gracious and blessed my choice. The next day I received unexpected news that a major part of my financial needs would be met. I just sat in wonder and amazement thinking, "God, you like me; you really do like me." It was one of those moments when I couldn't stop the tears; God thought more of me than I had thought of myself. He counted me worthy of support, and he had provided what was needed. I could only fall to my knees and raise my hands to him in thanksgiving. Even though I have failed many times, he was with me. I still am overwhelmed with how much he cares for me.

God's affirmation gives me courage and creates in me an intense desire to please him. It inspires me to risk, not to be afraid, not to hold back anything. This is exactly what Satan doesn't want—deeply loved, secure disciples fearlessly marching into his realm and taking people from him. Transformation begins in our thoughts; it is a total exchange of the flotsam and jetsam of the postmodern mind for the ideas of Christ. False ideas still exist, but they can be captured and disarmed. We can really think Christ's thoughts now. This is the life to which God has called us.

TRANSFORMED IMAGES

Images are the pictures in our mind's eye. They are concrete and often specific. The images that accompany our ideas make them more powerful. They are what the Lincoln Memorial is to liberty, what Lance Armstrong is to dedication, and what Elvis Presley is to self-indulgence. Just as images can be powerfully used for good, they can also magnify negatives. One's negative image of self can override clear thinking or any other force in life.

What Do You See in the Mirror?

How can a young, skinny girl look into the mirror and see fat? The once-great singer Karen Carpenter is entombed near my mother. When I walk by her burial site, I am reminded of her losing struggle with an eating disorder. She starved herself to death based on a false image. What she saw in the mirror was a lie, but that image had tremendous power. Karen's story is not about the image we would have seen if we stood behind her at the mirror. It is about what she saw based on her false belief.

Everyone has a self-image—a good one or a bad one, a true one or a false one. Let's say you grew up in a broken home or your parents were neglectful—the house was full but nobody was home. This can distort reality, and our culture gives you a pass on responsibility by labeling you a victim. You go through life as a wounded soul; it becomes your excuse, your reality, your self-image.

I did grow up in a broken home. My father abandoned my mother when my sister was still in the womb and I was a baby. There was an emptiness in my life as a boy. I acted out in school, and I fell behind in my work. I was rudely awakened at age twelve when I failed the seventh grade. The powerful image I carried was that I was dumb. I was known around the junior high as Billy "duh" Hull. I finished high school 411th out of 413 seniors, and I got the old Bronx cheer when I received my diploma.[8]

I went on to college on the best affirmative action program in the United States, the athletic scholarship. I carried with me the image of myself as a poor student. Freshman Composition had me reeling, but I studied and hung on. I was very resourceful, which is to say I cheated, and was able to graduate from the community college.

I went on to a university on yet another basketball scholarship. Within weeks I committed my life to Christ, and I made a commitment not to cheat. I read verses such as, "I can do everything through [Christ] who gives me strength" (Phil. 4:13). I looked into the mirror of God's Word and I didn't see Bill "duh" Hull; I saw a person in whom God believed and whom he would help get it done. By my senior year I had a 3.0 grade point average and had discovered I had a good mind. As I prepare my tenth book, I can only say that God changed the image in my mind. He knocked out the false image that I was dumb. Today I consider myself a writer, a person with conceptual gifts that have and continue to be used in service to God's kingdom.

Distorted Images

When your image of self becomes distorted, you don't think of yourself as an object of God's love. You have no place to stand and no place from which to make a stand against peer pressure, fads, group think, and mob hysteria.

One of the more tragic examples of this is teenage male suicide in Micronesia. In his national best-seller, *The Tipping Point*, Malcolm Gladwell explains that in the early 1960s suicide was

---

8. The Bronx cheer is to mock you for finally doing something right. This came from the infamous days of bad baseball teams. Whether it was the Yankees or the old Brooklyn Dodgers, when the final out was made in an inning when the opponents scored a lot of runs, people would ridicule their team's poor performance with a mock cheer.

virtually unknown on the islands of Micronesia. Then it began to rise steeply until in the 1980s there were more suicides per capita there than anywhere else in the world. In the United States the suicide rate for teens was 22 per 100,000. In Micronesia the rate was 160 per 100,000—seven times higher. This was triggered by a single teen named Sima who took his own life because his father yelled at him. Other young boys committed suicide when they saw their girlfriends with another boy or because their parents refused them spending money.[9] The boys all mimicked one another in the way they hung themselves, and their suicide notes were focused on wounded pride or self-pity more than depression. The suicide epidemic grew in power and influence; it was the thing to do when life threw you a challenge. The idea was that life isn't fair, so end it, get out, avoid working through it. The image that gave it power was hanging yourself to demonstrate how hurt you are. Punish others; make them sorry they ever hurt you or denied your desire.

The contagion of images has also been seen in the rash of school shootings from Columbine, Colorado, to San Diego, California, to Paducah, Kentucky. The dissemination of an idea with its accompanying image is catapulted to a wide audience through the media, music, film, art, and fashion. The black coats worn by the Columbine shooters, the film *Natural Born Killers*, gangster rap, and teenage fashion trends that expose too much or mimic the styles of icons of contemporary rebellion all promote harmful images.

The national fascination with rapper Eminem is an indication of the power of image. Through his music he encourages rebellion in the form of antisocial behavior and mannerisms. Bill O'Reilly puts it this way, "Eminem's lyrics justify immediate gratification on all levels. If your girlfriend does you wrong, kick her in the stomach. If your mother gives you a hard time, call her a dirty name. If you want to get high—go right ahead.

9. Malcolm Gladwell, *The Tipping Point: How Little Things Can Make a Big Difference* (Boston: Little, Brown & Co., 2002), 217.

Thus we now have ten year old boys calling little girls 'bitches.' We have thirteen year olds with tattoos and body piercing. We have poor children without parental guidance selling dope and carrying guns." O'Reilly concludes, "Sure, we've always had teenage rebellion in this country. But now the bar has been dropped to the lowest level in our nation's entertainment history. Now it is okay to rap about abusing women, smoking crack and solving problems with a gun."[10] The most disappointing fact is that the adult entertainment community celebrates Eminem as a voice expressing the rage and angst of the disenfranchised. This is the twisted logic of postmodern minds that see no connection between ideas, images, and behavior. There are no signposts; there are no directions. As Blamires says, it truly is a jungle.

Yet even the conventional and Christian worlds are influenced powerfully by image. Success is an idea about achievement, and achievement has accoutrements. You wear designer clothes and drive a status car with the gold package while closing a big deal on your mobile. You belong to the right clubs, vacation at the acceptable locations, and of course you have the right personal trainer to help trim the pounds from your last cruise. Your kids must have the latest rage or they will be diminished.

Even church attendance is based on image—we want to be where the action is. Going to churches is contagious; leaving churches is contagious. The idea is that God blesses through numerical growth, and the image that reinforces the idea is a large and thriving church. The falsehood of such a notion is not that a larger church would be more polished and effective but that more people with better talent is a sign of God's favor and that smaller churches with less people and talent are lacking God's blessing. So Christians rotate from one not-so-exciting venue to the new and more attractive option.

I try to keep my level of cynicism low on this issue, but the way many Christians make choices is so disappointing. Neil Postman's marvelous work, *Amusing Ourselves to Death*, delivers a deft blow:

10. Bill O'Reilly, *Long Beach Press Telegram*, 17 January 2003.

"In America God favors all those who possess both a talent and a format to amuse, whether they be preachers, athletes, entrepreneurs, politicians, teachers or journalists."[11] Our culture makes it that much harder to find the mind of Christ when the images of success are portrayed in programs such as *Seinfeld*, *Cheers*, and *Friends*, presenting pointless lives in a moral vacuum.

Peter's Distortion

Peter had an idea about the Messiah mixed with an image that caused him to misread God's will. He was sure that the Messiah would be proclaimed as such and would finally be welcomed by the establishment. This would mean a ticker-tape parade down Jerusalem Way with Jesus and the twelve apostles seated in convertibles soaking up the adulation that comes with victory. When Jesus told him this was not to be, Peter was so sure Jesus was wrong that he took him aside to correct him. "'Never, Lord!' he said, 'This shall never happen to you!' Jesus turned and said to Peter, 'Get behind me, Satan! You are a stumbling block to me; you do not have in mind the things of God, but the things of men'" (Matt. 16:22–23).

A wrong idea accompanied by a powerful image will distort discernment. This is why A. W. Tozer's statement is so relevant, "Whatever comes into your mind when you think about God is the most important thing about you."[12] This is why the transformation of the mind must include first our ideas and second the images that give them power.

Taking Every Idea and Image Captive

Reading, meditating on, and memorizing the Scriptures along with silence and solitude become the basis for all transformation. It is not all there is to the transformation process, but it is the basis, the cornerstone.

11. Neil Postman, *Amusing Ourselves to Death* (New York: Penguin, 1984), 5.
12. A. W. Tozer, *Knowledge of the Holy* (San Francisco: HarperSanFrancisco, 1998), 9.

Madame Guyon, a French writer who was imprisoned for twenty-five years in the Bastille because of her religious beliefs, wrote many books during those years. One that helped John Wesley, Hudson Taylor, Watchman Nee, and many others including myself is *Experiencing the Depths of Jesus Christ*.[13] Madame Guyon provided a way to pray the Scriptures and have them transform the mind. The following is an example of her advice.

1. Turn to a Scripture passage that is simple and practical.
2. Come to the Lord quietly and humbly.
3. Read a small portion.
4. Do not move on until you sense the very heart of what you have read.
5. Take that portion and turn it into prayer.
6. After you have exhausted the deeper sense and how it applies to you, move on to the next small section, a verse or two.

Madame Guyon went on to teach how to experience the presence of God. She used two illustrations that I found helpful. The first is the difference between a bee that skims the surface of a flower and the one that penetrates into the depths of the flower "You plunge deeply within to remove its deepest nectar." The second: "Have you at times enjoyed the flavor of a very tasty food? But unless you were willing to swallow the food, you received no nourishment. It is the same with your soul. In this quiet, peaceful, and simple state simply take in what is there as nourishment."[14]

The ideas that need to be transformed are deeply embedded, and so the Scriptures will need to go just as deep. I am guilty of reading the Bible only for information, to satisfy my cerebral needs. It is an acquired skill to go deep, to reroute the words

13. Madame Guyon, *Experiencing the Depths of Jesus Christ*, as recorded in *Devotional Classics: Selected Readings for Individuals and Groups*, ed. Richard Foster and James Bryan Smith (New York: HarperCollins, 1990).

14. Ibid., 320–23.

through the heart in prayer and reflection. So we rebuild the mind slowly, idea by idea, passage by passage until the ideas of Christ crowd out and replace the destructive fixtures that have held us captive. My prayer especially when stimulated by a crisis or major decision is, "Lord, what lies have I believed, what images of myself and others are distorted? Lord, bring down those strongholds." This prayer is best said on one's knees with an open Bible, for the answers lie in prayer and meditation on God's Word.

TRANSFORMED FEELINGS

Transformation of the mind begins with ideas, ideas are reinforced by images, and feelings are the product of both. Once set in place, feelings can be the most powerful force of all.

When transformation begins in the mind, the goal is the mind of Christ. That means we want to acquire the ideas of Christ and the images of Christ, and we want to feel what Jesus feels. My theology of feelings is that feelings or emotions are generated by the set structure of our ideas and their associated images.

An example of my theory comes from a well-known case involving a problem between siblings:

> Now Abel kept flocks, and Cain worked the soil. In the course of time Cain brought some of the fruits of the soil as an offering to the LORD. But Abel brought fat portions from some of the firstborn of his flock. The LORD looked with favor on Abel and his offering, but on Cain and his offering he did not look with favor. So Cain was very angry, and his face was downcast.
>
> Genesis 4:2–5

Abel's offering was superior because it came from his "firstborn"—it was his best. Cain's however, came from "some" of his fruits, but not the firstfruits that God requires. Cain became angry; he was depressed—in what we might call a fit or funk.

There are many schools of psychotherapy, and many of them would disconnect behavior from feeling. But God links them directly:

> Then the LORD said to Cain, "Why are you angry? Why is your face downcast? If you do what is right, will you not be accepted? But if you do not do what is right, sin is crouching at your door; it desires to have you, but you must master it."

> Genesis 4:6–7

God's counsel to Cain was, *if you do right, you will feel right.* Feelings are the product of right ideas and images connected to right behavior. Cain's actions were based on the wrong idea that he could please God on his own terms, supported by the image that God would smile upon him, which led to powerful feelings of rejection. Cain's expectations were not met, so he became angry and malice filled his heart. God told him what to do and warned him that if he didn't master his feelings and resist what he was thinking of doing, evil would have its way with him.

We have all at some time ignored instructions from a teacher and worked hard on a paper that didn't meet the requirements. We might have thought, "When the teacher sees how hard I worked and the quality of my paper, she will overlook that I wrote it on the wrong subject." When the teacher issued a failing grade, we got angry, even hostile. "Don't you realize how long and hard I worked on this? It's not fair that you won't reward my effort." Other students might have even smirked at our anger, which of course made us even angrier. So we went out and got drunk, dropped the class, and had to repeat it in summer school to graduate. Feelings are very powerful; they can and do overwhelm us. From Cain's murder of his brother to our dropping a class or shutting someone out, uncontrolled feelings can destroy us.

Uncontrollable Feelings

Feelings live on the front row of life like uncontrollable children competing for our attention. We've all had the experience of watching a touching scene in a film that evokes a feeling of sadness or joy. I have to admit that the scene in *Miss Congeniality* in which Sandra Bullock's character receives the Miss Congeniality award from her fellow contestants makes me cry every time. I hate myself for it; it is campy and ridiculous, but it moves me. We enjoy being moved. It feels good to have a good cry when the reason is positive; it actually feeds our souls. From *Sleepless in Seattle* to *Saving Private Ryan*, the tears flow throughout our land, and they are good and healing tears.

Willpower will not conquer feelings; we are almost helpless in their path. Many people think it is wrong to try to block or stuff our feelings, regardless of how ugly they may be. But Scripture offers a different way. Rather than try to control or stuff them, God actually says we can change them. He says we can feel about life what Jesus feels about life—that is transformation.

Slaying Passions and Desires

"Those who belong to Christ Jesus have crucified the sinful nature with its passions and desires" (Gal. 5:24). As we discussed earlier, there are two crucifixions. The first one we experienced mysteriously and passively in Christ when we entered into his provision of eternal life (Rom. 6:6). The second requires our active participation as we existentially live that first crucifixion day by day, taking every thought captive to Christ, working out what God has worked in us, and walking in the light and the Spirit (2 Cor. 10:3–5; Gal. 5:16–17; Eph. 5:15–6:4; Phil. 2:13; 1 John 1:3–9).

Passions and desires (also known as feelings) are the most used and powerful tools that trigger sinful action. That is why we are exhorted to put away such strong urges (Gal. 5:19–21; Eph. 4:31). Many sincere disciples suffer in their walk because they made commitments prompted by feelings. You walked off the job in anger or got married in a fever. A moment of passion led to pregnancy, you burned a relational bridge over a silly disagreement, or you said some things to friends that no one will be able to forget.

The young are often thought of as being dominated by feelings, but I can tell you that uncontrolled emotions devastate the aged as well. The young may have larger glandular excretions, but the aged have emotional structures that are hardened in place. There is nothing quite like the seriously seasoned saint's disgust as he stands in judgment of a skateboarding boy with his pants hanging below his butt as the boy skates his way to Bible study. People of all ages can be enslaved to their feelings of anger, anxiety, malice, rage, and bitterness.

Feelings as Servants

The primary work of the Spirit is that we desire not to sin. We desire to develop a passion to please God, and we want feelings that lead us away from sin. We want to be repulsed by rage, self-pity, and resentment. We want to discard being a slave to praise or to the feeling you get when you drink too much or to the rush you get doing the forbidden. What does it take to get to that point? The first word of the gospel is *repentance;* we must determine that we want change. To get us to repentance often takes desperation, hitting the bottom. Most of us can't envision what we would be like without our fear, our anger, our lust, or our wounds. But the good news is that our feelings can become our servants.

How would you like feelings such as contentment, peace, satisfaction, and compassion to rule your life? How about a sense of joy and humor, a delight in God? Healthy feelings are essential to a good life, but we must take care of our feelings—they don't just happen. Jesus asked a man who hadn't walked in thirty-eight years the crucial question, "Do you want to be healed?" (John 5:6 RSV). The lame man first gave an excuse of why he couldn't be healed, why he had been that way for so long. Are you ready to lay aside your excuses? I am sure they are very compelling since they have convinced you all these years that you couldn't change. But the question is still on the table, "Do you want to be healed? Have you been an emotional invalid long enough?" Here is what to do if you want to change:

1. Choose the life; choose to follow Jesus and be made whole. Repent of not believing you could change or not wanting to change.

2. Immerse yourself in the kind of spiritual disciplines that focus on feeding on the Scriptures—reading, memorization, meditation. Receive the Bible with humility. G. K. with him if he were stranded on an island. His answer, *Thomas' Guide to Practical Ship Building.* He reasoned that if trapped, he would want a way to get home. If you want to transform your mind, ideas, images, and feelings, you want the book that will show you how to get home—the Bible. Only the Word of God can renew your mind and bring about transformation. Be a person of the book, and like St. Augustine, "Take it and read; take it and read." Ask God to meet you there as you read it with a repentant heart. Cram your mind with the Scripture and let it crowd out every thought that sets itself against the truth of God.

3. Commit to work together with another person in mutual submission who has the same goal. Remember you are *training* to transform your mind; you have forsaken *trying* to transform your mind.

4. Visualize a person you can't love or can't forgive. Imagine yourself loving and forgiving that person as Jesus would. Don't hold back; we can have the mind of Christ. We can have his ideas, picture his images, and feel what he feels.

7

RELATIONSHIPS
AND THE LIFE

The greatest hermeneutic of the gospel is a community that seeks to live by it.[1]

—Lesslie Newbigin

Bill Thrall wrote, "To rise above and beyond your individual best, you need a certain kind of environment in which to live and work. Such an environment would nurture the integra-tion of heart and hand, word and deed, spirituality and everyday life. It would nourish your relationship with God and kindle your connections with those around you. This environment and the relationships it spawns would help you become the kind of

1. Lesslie Newbigin, *The Gospel in a Pluralistic Society* (Grand Rapids: Eerdmans, 1990).

leader whom others want to follow."[2] To be "the kind of leader whom others want to follow" is the yearning of my heart; it is what every leader wants. But it is not what every leader gets. It is not even what every leader knows about. I led for years not realizing what I didn't know.

Frustration and failure in leadership are often linked to low emotional intelligence. Competence is not enough; huge gifts will eventually not satisfy; character flaws will eventually find you out. Most leaders do not start out desiring to be the kind of person others want to follow. Many think, "It's not about my inner life; it's about what I can do." Most young leaders start out expecting people to follow them because of their vision and skills—at least that is how I started. But when my skills failed me and it all caught up to me, I felt helpless.

Since my concept of leadership was vision, skills, and effective infrastructure, I underplayed the role of character. Character was nice to have, but it didn't get things done. I saw great people with sterling character who couldn't accomplish what I needed to do. The majority of leadership seminars and books are on competence, skills, and strategy. But there is a better way—to lead by influence of character.

THE LEGACY

A pastoral colleague told me that regardless of what I do from now on, my legacy will be disciple making. What he meant was that my books on disciple making have touched more lives than my pastoral work. Being known as a successful writer is fulfilling, and to be honored for creating something that helps others is one of the great rewards of life. It is thrilling to have a pastor tell me how my books have changed his life. If I entered the great beyond today, I would be happy to be remembered as a writer, but there is something even more important about Bill Hull.

2. Bill Thrall, Bruce McNicol, and Ken McElrath, *The Ascent of a Leader* (San Francisco: Jossey-Bass, 1999), 1.

The writing speaks to my perseverance, drive, and ability to think, but it leaves out my personal influence on others. As I like to tell my friends, it is wonderful to be honored but even better to be loved. An even more important legacy than my writing is Bill Hull the person and how other people experience me. So my intermittent pastoral work is another measure of my character; it reveals the product of my writing.[3]

What is my character? Does the fruit of the Spirit grow in me? Am I being transformed? I have come to believe that the primary and exclusive work of the church is spiritual transformation. That is about a change in which our character is being transformed into the image of Christ. And that character is formed in community, not in isolation. It is formed in the friction of living with others in covenant and then being tested in isolation.[4]

We lead out of our character even more than our skills. Competence and charisma have their place, but they fall in line behind character. I painfully discovered that if I wanted to be the kind of person whom others wanted to follow, it would require character transformation. I would need to really practice following Jesus rather than trying to lead him.

THE DISCIPLESHIP CLIMATE

One of the reasons that the disciple-making movement has languished is that the disciple-making climate has been

3. "Intermittent" meaning that twenty of the thirty-four years I have been in vocational ministry have been pastoral. It has been the seedbed from which my life's message has been developed for the church. The mission to return the church to its disciple-making roots has been the driving force of every expression of my work. The mission has had a pastoral element, but it is broader than the pastoral.

4. I am deeply indebted to Bill Thrall and Bruce McNicol, chairman and president (respectively) of Leadership Catalyst, for the concepts I am sharing. They taught me the concepts; they encouraged me to live them; and I experienced the joy of their fruit in my own community of faith. I will cite specific quotations from them, but I must also give them credit for the general flow of thought in this chapter. For a fuller understanding, please see Thrall, McNicol, and McElrath, *The Ascent of a Leader*, a groundbreaking work on the relational environment necessary for transformation.

largely ignored. The classic disciple-making movement has been strong in content and structure. Structure is not bad; in fact it is absolutely necessary for people to grow. You can't "teach people to obey everything Christ commanded" without structure. But structure is a means to an end, not the end itself. When structure becomes the end, it kills authentic spiritual life. It also allows people to perform year after year and accomplish all the program goals while avoiding the hidden issues that stunt their growth. When discipleship progress is measured by program completion, then failure is not finishing the program. Therefore, legalism's dirty hand takes hold of the believer's heart, because the goal is completion instead of personal transformation.

Much good has been done through the content and structure approach, but it has lacked the depth and mystical element in the faith that the historic spiritual formation movement has provided. Spiritual formation has been largely a product of the monastery and the academy, but now it is coming out of those closed environments and is joining forces with the classic disciple-making movement. The piece that forms the tour de force is the addition of the environmental or climatic movement, which says people only accept truth they trust. And that trust is only present when the faith community experiences relationships of trust in an environment of grace.[5] I believe this combination created by the Holy Spirit will sweep the nation and transform the church in America.

The revolutionary aspect to the movement of God that I have spoken of above is explained in figure 1. The classic disciple-making movement has been very strong on *principles*, but they have been experienced by many nonregimented personalities as ungracious and out of reach. Even mavericks require structure, but establishing the right *environment* will determine if they will join in.

The reason that most often engagement in serious discipleship

5. "Relationships of trust" and "environment of grace" are concepts created by Bill Thrall and Bruce McNicol of Leadership Catalyst.

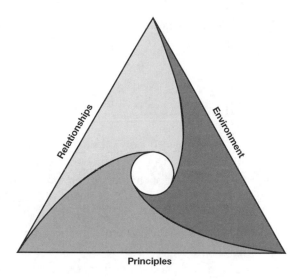

Principles

FIGURE 1. THE INTERDEPENDENCE OF ENVIRONMENT, RELATIONSHIPS, AND PRINCIPLES

Illustration from Bill Thrall, Bruce McNicol, and Ken McElrath, *The Ascent of a Leader* (San Francisco: Jossey-Bass, 1999), 35. Copyright © 1999. Reprinted by permission of John Wiley & Sons, Inc. and Leadership Catalyst, Inc.

has been limited to the few is because discipleship has been pro-gram based rather than rooted in *relationships* of trust. However, it should be stated here that programs that are relationally based are good and healthy because instead of measuring success by completed homework they measure fruit such as self-control or submission as an evidence of the filling of the Holy Spirit (Gal. 5:22–23; Eph. 5:21).

The third side of the triangle, *environment*, has too often been based on performance and results. There is nothing wrong with performance and results, but they must be set in the proper con-text of interdependence. Other churches are relationally driven to a fault and do not understand or adhere to a set of principles. The church can also become overly focused on psychology—on what we feel we want rather than on a set of principles that God tells us will meet our needs.

For a healthy environment, there must be a balance of prin-ciples and relationships that combine to create an environment of grace. This is an environment in which people are affirming to one another, where it is safe to risk, and in which great things are accomplished.

THE NEED FOR A HEALTHY CLIMATE

In my travels I have noticed how climate determines what thrives. In Ecuador I found that varmints thrive. I stayed at a "resort" on the beautiful coast of this very poor country. It looked like a resort when you gazed out to sea—the white sand and gorgeous colors of sky and water were as beautiful as anywhere in the world. But as you turned to look on shore you saw the primitive accommodations.

One night we were attacked by thousands of huge crickets; they were enormous and frightening, and they were everywhere. I went to my room to escape. I closed my door and shoved a towel around the bottom to keep them out. When I turned around, there were at least twenty of them in my room. I killed them all with my flip-flops, feeling a bit conflicted about the carnage. Once I was finally nestled into bed, I felt something moving. I raised my covers to find three more crickets that were planning on sleeping with me. I jumped out of bed and proceeded to end their lives.

Spiders and supersized crickets thrive in the hotels and homes of that tropical climate. If you travel to the Arctic there are no crickets or spiders, but polar bears and seals thrive. A few years later my experience in Saudi Arabia demonstrated that very little can naturally survive in that desert environment except lizards and golf. Yes, I lived across the street from a Saudi golf course for two days and didn't know it was a golf course. The fairways were sand marked with white lines; the greens were rolled sand. The golfer would tee off a patch of indoor/outdoor carpet, then take the carpet along in the cart. Wherever the ball landed, the golfer laid his ball on the carpet and played. I thought, "This would improve my game at home;

you always get a good lie." Golf could exist in Saudi Arabia but not thrive. In the same way, discipleship and transformation can survive in a legalistic and harsh climate but not thrive.

In what climate does transformation thrive? The answer is simple: In order for anyone to grow, there must be a safe, risk-free environment.[6] Repentance and confession are linked to trust in others. Can I be real? Can I be vulnerable? Can I submit myself to these people? Unless the community provides a safe environment that promotes trust, people will not open up. Unless people open up, transformation will be largely absent, which explains a lot of the problems the church is facing.

In *Interpersonal Competence and Organizational Effectiveness* C. Argyris says, "Without interpersonal competence or a psychologically safe environment, the organization is a breeding ground for mistrust, intergroup conflict, rigidity and so on, which lead to a decrease in organizational success in problem solving."[7] The institutionalized church reflects this reality. A typical scenario goes something like this: The church is short of money, so the trustees try to tighten up and control the staff. The trustees get increasingly rigid and judgmental, and they start to grab power for the good of the church. The staff begin to bristle and then rebel. The elders are called in to referee the fight, and everyone is bewildered, wondering how they got into this mess. So the focus becomes who is right and who is wrong. When locked in a relational firestorm like this, thinking of spiritual transformation is nearly impossible.

This scenario is much too common because we have not built safe and affirming environments. There is a trust gap, and people are transformed only by the truth they trust.[8] What could cause the trustees, staff, and elders to drop their guard and in humility submit to one another and change from an institutional com-

6. Thrall, McNicol, and McElrath, *The Ascent of a Leader*, chap. 11.
7. C. Argyris, *Interpersonal Competence and Organizational Effectiveness* (Homewood, Ill.: Dorsey Press and Irwin, 1962), 43.
8. Bill Thrall and Bruce McNicol, *Forming the High-Trust Culture* (Leadership Catalyst, 2000), A-16, A-17.

munity to a relational community? The most effective way for me to answer that question is to explain how it happened to me.

MY TRANSFORMATION EXPERIENCE

I spent the first fifty years of my life climbing what Leadership Catalyst calls the Capacity Ladder (see fig. 2). I discovered what I could do early in my life. I could sell and persuade people to adopt my position. At nine years of age I sold more newspaper subscriptions to the *Indianapolis Times* than any other newspaper boy in the city. As a result I won a trip by train to the Queen City to see my heroes, the Cincinnati Reds. In 1966 at age twenty, I was making three hundred dollars a week selling radio advertising as a summer job. As newlyweds in 1969, Jane and I joined the Athletes in Action basketball team, and I was able to raise our required financial support in two weeks.

FIGURE 2. THE PORTABLE CAPACITY LADDER

Illustration from Bill Thrall, Bruce McNicol, and Ken McElrath, *The Ascent of a Leader* (San Francisco: Jossey-Bass, 1999), 46. Copyright © 1999. Reprinted by permission of John Wiley & Sons, Inc. and Leadership Catalyst, Inc.

I have a history of being able to combine focus, determination, and discipline to reach a specific goal. The first time this gift or trait was not as welcome was my first year as a pastor. It became clear to me that people in a religious community were not as concerned about measurable progress as I was.

Importance of Character

In my first church there was a retired man named Wally Lentz. A petite man, thin and wiry with a whisper of a voice. He spent most weekdays volunteering his time around the church as a gardener and handyman. It didn't matter what needed to be done, if he knew how, he would do it. Wally was one of the few who were willing to go door-to-door with me. His life was impeccable, his attitude was one of great humility. If you had asked anyone in the church to describe a godly man, each one would have pointed at Wally.

Wally's sacrificial attitude, his humility, and his walk with God all made him the most influential man in the church. He had power over all of us, yet he rarely spoke. He saved most of his words for when he was telling people about Christ. Wally was the first common man I had met who demonstrated great power through his character. I appreciated and admired Wally's influence, but at the time I didn't fully comprehend that if Wally had disagreed with me, the church would have followed him. So I went on my way to advance to a larger church still not understanding character and its influence in sufficient depth to change my style.

Over the years I accomplished enough and went from one project to another often enough to avoid confronting my character flaws. By the time I was fifty I had moved up to the top of the Capacity Ladder (see fig. 2). I had discovered what I could do and had developed my capacities to communicate with both the spoken and written word. I was a published author of several groundbreaking books and had acquired title and position in my world.

I recall having lunch with a friend one day discussing what God had done through us. He mentioned that I had already accomplished more than most men, that at fifty I had attained my individual potential. I was standing on the top rung of the

Capacity Ladder. Most people believed me to be a person of high personal character, I was a growing disciple, and God was using me. But I had no idea what God had in store for me in the next five years.

Although character is developed on the Capacity Ladder, there is a Character Ladder (see fig. 3), and it has more rails and is much taller than the Capacity Ladder. The Character Ladder begins with humility, then submission, obedience, suffering, and finally exaltation. Why would anyone willingly climb this ladder? The only answer is a desire to follow Christ.

Environments of grace		Relationships of grace
	Discover my identity	
	Suffering/maturity	
	Pay the price	
	Obedience	
	Align with truth	
	Submission	
	Choose vulnerability	
	Humility	
	Trust God and others with me	

FIGURE 3. THE CHARACTER LADDER

Illustration from Bill Thrall, Bruce McNicol, and Ken McElrath, *The Ascent of a Leader* (San Francisco: Jossey-Bass, 1999), 140. Copyright © 1999. Reprinted by permission of John Wiley & Sons, Inc. and Leadership Catalyst, Inc.

What I discovered was that when I took on a pastoral role, I had stepped off the top of the Capacity Ladder and moved to the middle of the Character Ladder. God had more things for me to do, but first he wanted to develop characteristics in me that would prepare me for the work. So he placed me in the middle of a community. I had been living a life of hundreds of friends and thousands of admirers but no one speaking into my life, no one to whom I submitted. Please remember that character is developed in community, then tested in isolation. So God was saying, "Climb, Bill, climb the ladder."

Humility, Even Humiliation

At first I lived off reputation and ministered out of my head. For over ten years no one had expected anything pastoral from me. I was the exhorter, the expert, the writer who could say things to the church their pastor would not dare utter. The outside prophet is a hero; the inside prophet usually has many wounds. Initially people in my church were very pleased with my competence and skill, my preaching and planning. They saw me as someone who knew more about churches than any pastor they had before, and I was older and more experienced, so people deferred to me, believing that my plans would bring great success. I was still traveling a good amount and calling churches to return to their disciple-making roots.

The first sign of trouble was the reaction to the display of my then eight published books in a prominent area in the church lobby. It wasn't my idea, but I agreed it would be nice for the congregation to know what I had written. I was shocked and hurt by the response of many who thought I was self-promoting and wanted the display taken down. I first thought they were being petty and even jealous. Why was it okay to rejoice with singing groups over their first CD or celebrate a boy becoming an Eagle Scout or another person's acting or poetry but not my books?

A second issue arose concerning music. Many of the older members had been complaining about it for years and were hoping that since I was older I would return the church to a more traditional worship style. The leadership thought we should be real clear that we were not going to regress, so at my first annual meeting of the congregation I made the following statement: "I know many of you want to return to a more traditional worship, but I want you to know that is not going to happen. We have discussed it and prayed about it, and so I think it would be wise for you to stop complaining. Complaining is not only a sin, it also won't do any good. The case is closed; we will not revisit this anymore." That was my best attempt to speak the tough love to the congregation that staff and elders hadn't had the courage to do.

As I look back on these two episodes, I see that I was operating out of my head more than my heart. My heart was involved, and I felt very deeply about everything; it just wasn't getting through to people. Because I wasn't connecting, they didn't rejoice with my success (the book display), and they took offense at my statement about the future of our worship.

Dependence on Competence Had to Go

I had several experiences over the next few months that became a transformational elixir prescribed by God. I went to England for two weeks of teaching at a very large conference. The stated reason for my being there was to solve the "Who is Bill Hull?" problem in the United Kingdom, which was an important step to a long-range ministry plan. But when I arrived, all the prearranged agreements were forgotten or had not been communicated. I spent the two weeks in relative obscurity, and I practiced humility by not complaining or insisting on the fulfillment of the agreement concerning speaking assignments.

Not long after that, some people in the church began to complain about my teaching, and some even left the church. Over the years there had been people who couldn't handle my preaching style, but they had always been replaced by many more who loved it. But this time the people were not talking about my competence; they were talking about an emotional connection. I am passionate, but I get excited about ideas. These people saw me as emotionally aloof; they sensed that I couldn't feel their pain. I began to experience rejection—a lot of people were not able to connect with me and decided to go somewhere else. What made it worse were the comments, "Your sermons are really good, but something is missing," or, "We like you very much, but you are not connecting with us."

Many also rejected my vision and became resistant to change. Some of this is the human condition and happens everywhere, but for me it was part of a bigger picture. So the great plans and strategies rolled right off them, and a cynicism set in that all these plans were just what leadership wanted and no one was listening to the people. The fact that we had no net church growth kept the issues alive. The pity is if the nickels and noses would have doubled, I could have been mean-spirited or even cavalier about people's leaving, and they would have called me a brave prophet for our time.

A Transformational Community

I decided to attend a four-day conference that was designed to help people learn how others experience them. Four days is a big commitment, but a good number of people in our church had attended, so I decided to give it a whirl. I went into it with a prayer, "Lord, I am not against any change you want to make in my life." After all, God loves me and understands me better than I do; any change he wants to make is good. During my times of prayer I heard that whisper from him, "Bill, I'm going to break you. Don't run." That is not what I wanted to hear, but I committed myself to it.

The seminar was characterized by exercises in which we learned how we relate to others. The days were long and demanding both physically and emotionally. The environment was not immediately one of grace; it was one of uncertainty, fear of exposure, and risk. The fifty-four people in the room were on a level playing field. Being a medical doctor, a pastor, or a successful businessperson didn't count, and for the most part we did not learn what the others did for a living until the end of our time together. It revealed how accustomed I was to having a status advantage in relationships by being clergy and a published author. I was stripped down to the real me, and people judged me by what they experienced of me.

Toward the end of the second day, each person went around the room telling every person face-to-face whether they thought that person was a giver or a taker. It was a somber exercise; you were at the mercy of the group opinion based only on how they had experienced you for two days. Many looked me straight in the eye and said, "Taker." I was mildly offended, thinking, "These people don't know who I am, and this is make-believe.

They don't look that smart to me. Don't they realize I'm giving my valuable time to be with them?"

The next day we formed a U with our chairs and were seated according to the group's evaluation. The most giving person was in seat one; the biggest taker was in seat fifty-four. I was in seat fifty. The only consolation was that my wife was in seat fifty-two, and after thirty years of marriage I considered her the most giving person I had ever known.

I was in seat fifty not because I had been mean and nasty; I was there because I had spent two days holding back. I was holding back because I was not going to dirty myself by submitting to the artificial nature of the seminar. I considered much of what I heard there to be pathetic, other parts ridiculous, but some of it was real and powerful. I was holding back because down deep I thought I was above them, not as needy and ridiculous. My pride kept me from giving myself to them. I sat back and refused to engage, which seemed selfish to the group, and I now believe they were right.

When it came out that I was a pastor, one woman didn't hold back, "How can you be a pastor and be sitting there?"—referring to my place in seat fifty. The facilitator followed up, "That's a good question. Bill, why are you there? What is this about?"

That was when it hit me: This is why I don't connect with some people who leave our church. It is why my skills fall short, why excellent sermons don't connect, why people don't take hold of the vision. I am holding myself back from them. I realized I had been emitting an odor of condescension and smugness. I didn't feel it consciously, but it was coming through. That was the breaking point for me; I realized that my love sounded like clanging pots and pans (1 Cor. 13:1–6).

Jesus Did Not Hold Back

That four-day conference was the first time I really understood that I was not loving as Jesus loved. Jesus didn't hold back; I did. Jesus gave himself to people who didn't respond to his ministry; I didn't. Jesus was willing to sacrifice his own desires to get the job done; I wasn't. I was broken into pieces when I understood this, and it opened up a whole new world for me.

God never breaks us like we break things. We break things accidentally or we destroy things in anger or despair. Rarely do we break things in order to improve them. But when God breaks us he does it gently and then puts it back together again.

Not long ago my wife led a workshop called "Trash to Treasure." Jane asked women to bring to the workshop dishes that they wouldn't mind breaking. She had women break the dishes they had brought along and then they proceeded to take plaster and make mosaics out of what was broken. As they worked, Jane told them she had broken her favorite dish from her precious Blue Willow collection as a metaphor regarding the smashed dreams we had for our oldest son, who had gone through a period of gut-wrenching rebellion for reasons we still don't fully understand. When Jane told the women her story, the tears flowed. They were all deeply moved, and most could relate to losing something so precious but then seeing God put those shattered dreams back together again.

The world is filled with broken people who have been smashed by the world, and they remain bitter, angry, or proud. When God breaks us it is only to bring humility into our lives, and then he puts us back together in his grace.

When God broke me that evening in the conference, I made a commitment to love as Jesus loved. I wouldn't hold back; I would find a way to get through to others. Jesus loves us until we get it that he loves us, which is the only reason the church exists. God was still loving me as he was in the process of breaking me. He had used the artificial environment of the conference, and it had served its purpose. Now I had to reenter my normal community.

BACK TO THE REAL COMMUNITY

The real community in which I live is not artificial; it is not short-term. It is like family, and it is where I need to love. After the conference, I had a week to prepare my next sermon, and I knew it would need to be about what God had taught me. I was ready to climb to the next rung of the ladder; I was going to make a commitment that would require my submission to the people. This was a transformational moment. Such moments don't happen often, but recognizing them opens the community to progress. Transformational moments can be a communal crisis such as when the church burns down or when members are unexpectedly taken through death. In this case the community leader was in a serious life change that would be painful. And that pain needed to be shared.

I trembled with fear many times before I preached my early sermons. But I have only trembled once as a seasoned communicator, and it was that Sunday and that sermon. Confession may be good for the soul, but it is lousy for the ego. I don't recall the outline or text, but I can remember my tears, their tears, and the looks on their faces. And I will never forget their response.

First I told them that my goal was to be the kind of leader others wanted to follow based on their perception of my character.[9] They needed to experience my love, which meant my love had to go beyond intellectual assent. It had to be a commitment on my part to find a way to love them as Jesus loved—a commitment to break through all barriers until they could truly experience my love.

I took them into my inner world and told them about the rejection of my father and the love of my mother. I had put up a wall to separate myself from the emotion of my father never wanting to meet me or know about me. I had lived a life of building walls to separate myself from pain and rejection. As a result I protected myself from people by withholding my heart, unwilling to place my heart on the altar.

Then I shared with them my mother's story—a newly married teenage girl living out a dream come true. There she was on the back of a Harley Davidson with her arms locked around the

9. Thrall, McNicol, and McElrath, *The Ascent of a Leader,* chaps. 11–12.

waist of her strapping, six-foot four-inch husband. It was 1945, the war was over, and her soldier boy was whisking her away from the strict religion and judgment of her central Indiana home to his rich father's mansion in Beverly Hills. He looked like Errol Flynn, and sadly it turned out he lived like the womanizing Flynn. Within weeks she was pregnant with me and on a train back to Indiana to her parents' home. There was a short reconciliation, but only long enough for my sister to become a reality. Then he was off again to his California home, never to be heard from again.

It was an amazing revelation that when I tore down the wall that protected me from my own pain of rejection, for the first time I felt my mother's pain. It rushed over me with such power. I could feel her joy of being rescued from a dull and drab life, but I could sense the disappointment, rejection, and shame of coming home to a rigid and judgmental mother who made sure the girl understood that all her problems came from not listening to her mother. My mother never married again; she raised her son and daughter with grace and dignity. I sobbed as I told this story, feeling deeper emotions than ever in my life.

Then it was time to take the plunge. I paused and then said it, "I make a commitment to you today; I will love you in such a way that you will experience my love. I will not hold back. Like my Leader, Jesus, I will find a way to reach you. I will accept that some people can't be reached because they refuse to accept love from others. I will also accept my limitations and circumstances beyond my control. But any failure to connect will not be from a lack of my personal commitment to love others."

My tears seeded theirs, which flowed freely, and they came forward in great numbers to pray. They got it; they heard me; I had broken through. Humility and confession had won the day. God punched a big hole in my wall; I stepped through it, and they met me there. They had received my truth, and it had touched them deeply. They trusted it, so they accepted it.

DOWN THE MOUNTAIN INTO THE STREETS OF REALITY

That moment transformed my relationship with the people. It was strong and lasting in the new way I was talking with them and relating to them. Emotion is essential to change, but it cannot carry the full load of corporate transformation. The moment was like creating a new document on your computer with new fonts and settings. But once you close that document, all future documents revert to the default position. Any group of people have their default settings, habits, and patterns that are resistant to change. We had that moment on the mountain, but now we had to descend to the streets of reality.

Keep Climbing, Bill

I was now climbing the Ladder of Success (fig. 4), which is a combination of the ladders of capacity and character. I found myself standing on the rung "Acquire positions that match who I am" with one hand firmly on the rung above me, "Pay the price." God was about to field test my new commitment.

FIGURE 4. THE LADDER OF SUCCESS

Illustration from Bill Thrall, Bruce McNicol, and Ken McElrath, *The Ascent of a Leader* (San Francisco: Jossey-Bass, 1999), 144. Copyright © 1999. Reprinted by permission of John Wiley & Sons, Inc. and Leadership Catalyst, Inc.

A couple weeks later was our church leadership retreat. My stated goal had become to transform our church from an institutional community to a relational one. We leaders were to be examples to the flock, and I was charged with being the leader of personal transformation. So I designed the retreat to be relational first and decision making second. Friday night we spent time affirming one another. It was a hit. The leaders were so encouraged, and we broke through several barriers. There was laughter and tears, hugs all around, and many commented it was the best group experience of their lives. They had a taste of what God had been doing in me and some others on the pastoral staff.

I then encouraged them to be as open and vulnerable as I had been. What then came out was not a surprise if one is analyzing a group of leaders from afar. But when you are being swept along in the current of emotion, it is a shock to your system.

I recommended that all our leaders attend the same seminar that had been so transformational in my life. The leaders thought the experience was a great thing for me and really good for the church, but they were not prepared to climb the ladder of transformation with me. Some were open, but then a controversy arose. The creator of the seminar had some New Age associations in the early years. But by the time I participated in the seminar, it had been refined and tested, and I had found it biblical. But some of our leaders started reading critical analysis by a few people who reported other people's bad experiences. This was an honest inquiry and was done in good faith. They had done it with a legitimate motive to protect the flock.

I had wanted to expose more of our people to the principles and experiences that had helped me. I am convinced that participation in this behavioral learning laboratory would have advanced our transition from an institutional community to a relational community. Instead, the inquiry led to a very grievous difference of opinion and a divided elder board. We could not come to agreement; instead, we had to compromise to maintain unity on the larger issues. And may I add, there may not be any larger issues. Unfortunately, some of the elders chose to believe the internet critics instead of three of their pastors. So the process that had done so much to change my life was rejected by some of our leaders. The irony was that some of the same people who wanted me to change rejected the process that brought about change in my life and insisted that no one else in our church hear about it. So I wanted a transformational community, relationally driven, and based on trust, but trust had just been shattered due to mistrust and fear.

RELATIONSHIPS OF TRUST

Why do people stop trusting each other? Trust is built on integrity; integrity is a commitment to truth regardless of circumstances.[10] Disagreement doesn't destroy trust; rather, trust is destroyed by the avoidance of honest, forthright interaction. Many are afraid of living in the light relationally, and that fear leads to treachery, talking about people instead of with them, avoidance of tough issues, and withholding true feelings in order to avoid conflict. So people live under a false impression that we agree with them when all along we just didn't want to tell them the truth. That is how trust is destroyed.

Why is Jesus trustworthy? Because he told the truth and lived the truth. Jesus made promises and kept them even though it cost him friends, family, national acceptance, and his life. Jesus was honest with everyone: Nicodemus, the woman at the well, the rich young ruler, his mother and brothers, Peter, and the other disciples. He was brutally honest, even confrontational with religious leaders. Yet this sometimes painful truth came from a man who was the epitome of trustworthiness and integrity. Jesus' character inspired others to follow him and give their lives as well. That is why spiritual leaders are to be examples to the flock (1 Peter 5:1–6).

10. Thrall, McNicol, and McElrath, *The Ascent of a Leader*, chap. 6.

The sacrifice I was called to make was to build back the trust that had been lost. This was not a matter of people speaking truth or falsehood; it was about trusting each other's spirituality and wisdom. Jesus said,

> No good tree bears bad fruit, nor does a bad tree bear good fruit. Each tree is recognized by its own fruit. People do not pick figs from thornbushes, or grapes from briers. The good man brings good things out of the good stored up in his heart, and the evil man brings evil things out of the evil stored up in his heart. For out of the overflow of his heart his mouth speaks.
>
> Luke 6:43–45

Bearing good fruit meant that I was to love them as Christ loved them. Although deeply wounded that they had not believed my testimony, I had to put the pain of rejection behind me. I was influenced by the words of Thomas à Kempis, "Be not angry that you cannot make others as you wish them to be, since you cannot make yourself as you wish to be."[11] My role was to submit to the elders, to humble myself before them and not act out or abuse my pastoral authority and platform to seek revenge. The proof of my transformation was to be the good fruit from my life—the fruit that comes from following the example of Jesus.

There were many days I had to bite my tongue. Some members agreed with some of the elders, but unlike the elders, they felt free to say hurtful things about me and then left the church. Many other members heard about the decision and wanted to take on my pain. It can be so comforting to have people sympathize with your wound, but I resisted the temptation and told them that would be wrong because I knew that the quality of character is what would elicit trust from others.

11. Thomas à Kempis, *The Imitation of Christ*, in *A Guide to Prayer for Ministers and Other Servants*, comp. Rueben P. Job and Norman Shawchuck (Nashville: Upper Room, 1983), 113.

The Relational Community

You will notice that the Ladder of Success has two rails: relationships of trust and environments of grace (see fig. 4). Relationships require trust because trust is the prerequisite to submission. Without submission I cannot practice humility, and without humility I will not allow you to speak into my life. And without that vulnerability, transformation won't happen. This is why "God opposes the proud but gives grace to the humble" (1 Peter 5:5). Pride blocks the communication of truth and builds walls that doom a community to superficial relationships. I knew that I would need to humble myself before the leaders and congregation and allow them to speak into my life. My announcement was simple, "I am not against any change God wants to make in my life. I am the lucky one; I get to lead in changing."

It all sounded good, but we had so little experience in helping each other keep our commitments to God. Open, honest relationships terrify most people. The easiest thing to do is criticize others but not to talk to them. Most statements are passed along until they eventually get back to the person criticized. This generates bad feelings, malice, bitterness, and other emotional garbage. Then the relationships are broken, walls are constructed, and the transformation is not into the image of Christ but into the defeated believer who has no deep, accountable relationships.

I Am Going to Trust You with Me

The only way I knew to develop relationships of trust was to submit myself to others by faith and give them permission to speak into my life. I told them, "I am going to trust you with me." I will never forget the expressions on the faces as they softened. Because they trusted what I said and received it as true, it created change in them. They started coming to me and telling me how they needed to do the same thing; elders joined me at the altar for prayer. The barriers broke down, and we were on our way to a relational community because now many were willing to climb the ladder with me.

I knew that if we could get our small groups, the one-on-one relationships, and even our middle-size groups to start with mutual submission, we could start taking back relational ground from the Enemy. The way the church is supposed to work is that we experience the influence of other people in our lives through mutual submission. God has gifted so many around us, but our pride and fear block their love. Spiritual gifts are God present with us through other believers, which is how God has designed the body to meet each other's needs. That is why relationships of trust at the leadership level are the basis for the entire congregation to experience God's very best. That causes people to come out of their shells and risk telling you what they are really like—their fears, troubles, and challenges. This positions them for change, for transformation. Without relationships of trust we are sentenced to discipleship programs with no punch; the principles and activities roll off the believer's back like the proverbial water off the duck.

It was clear we were on our way when the relational defenses came down and we leaders started treating each other like brothers with needs instead of role players with job descriptions. When leaders model and communicate authentic relationships, it is a powerful tool for God to use.

ENVIRONMENT OF GRACE

Relationships of trust establish the environment of grace that best makes disciples. There is an old story about a little boy trying to get a turtle to come out of its shell. He yelled at it, poked his finger under the shell, tried to pull on the turtle's head, and even threw it to the ground in frustration. I have often thought this is the way we have tried to get people to go deeper with God and practice the spiritual disciplines. Too often we exhort, cajole, or hammer people with Scripture to make them feel lousy. It is an approach based on our shortcomings and failures. "How can we expect to know God and be fruitful when we don't fast, spend hours alone with God, etc.?" It is like the boy's poking and yelling—it makes most of us retreat into our protective shells.

When acceptance is performance-based, people will hide and play it safe rather than take risks. Effort and performance are essential in order to follow Christ, but they are to be the fruit of acceptance that is based on the body modeling God's grace.

If people feel safe, we will take risks and come out of our shells. When the boy's sister came along, she placed the harassed turtle into the warmth and safety of her gentle hand. She stroked the turtle's shell and held it close to the fire and waited patiently. A short time later the turtle emerged into an environment more to his liking.

An environment of grace is a safe place in which people are encouraged to live out the dream God has for them. An environment of grace is where we are accepted for who we are. That doesn't mean we are not expected to grow and develop—quite the opposite. It is only when we sense acceptance that we will lower our defenses and walk in the light, admitting our needs and allowing others to help us. That is when we will "trust others with me."

I can't say it too strongly, "trusting others with me" is the essence of discipleship; it is what leads to inner change. Because we have neglected the environment that leads to transformation, we have a nation of stuck believers who have retreated to mediocrity and defeat, still overeating, still racked with anxiety, still strangled by debt and not able to tithe. And most importantly, they still are not spending fruitful time with God, and as a result they are living out a puny little version of what God had in mind for them (Eph. 2:10).

C. S. Lewis described it so powerfully: "Indeed, if we consider the unblushing promises of reward and the staggering nature of the rewards promised in the Gospels, it would seem that our Lord finds our desires not too strong, but too weak. We are half-hearted creatures, fooling about with drink and sex and ambition when infinite joy is offered us, like an ignorant child who wants to go on making mud pies in a slum because he cannot imagine what is meant by the offer of a holiday at the sea. We are too easily pleased."[12]

An environment of grace is a community in which disciples accept each person where they are, celebrate how God has made them, and encourage each other to train to be godly. Relationships are messy and we will get hurt, but they are absolutely crucial to personal development because we can't mature in isolation. We all have basic needs such as security, significance, acceptance, and attention. God designed us to be loved by a God of love, and he very often meets our needs through the body of believers. That is why an environment of grace celebrates our strengths and protects our weaknesses. It is fueled by affirmation.

Affirmation

Affirmation is a love word that ministers to the heart.[13] Praising others is not the strength of many. Evangelicals in particular tend to retreat from affirming others because it might give someone a "big head." This is part of our twisted theology that has created environments of critique. In fact the most natural inclination is to critique those around us. The reason for this is that most of us are affirmation starved, so we knock down others in order to feel a bit better about ourselves. The apostle Paul disagrees with those who think critique is the best environment: "Let no corrupt communication proceed out of your mouth, but what is good for necessary edification, that it may impart grace to the hearers" (Eph. 4:29 NKJV).

Affirmation imparts grace; in other words, it is a gift to the recipient. Affirmation is an act of love, and love never arouses sin; instead it arouses the desire to please God.[14] I know when people affirm my gift for teaching, it makes me want to do even

---

12. C. S. Lewis, *The Weight of Glory*, in *A Guide to Prayer*, 85.
13. Thrall and McNicol, *Forming the High-Trust Culture*, 3–4.
14. Ibid.

better, to work harder. When people have told me they notice that I am more caring, it makes me want to be even more so. Then why is it that as a pastor I had hesitated to praise the congregation for their excellent giving? Because deep down I believed that they would reduce their giving if they thought we were doing well financially. My first thought was their depravity, not their sacrificial natures, which reveals how deep this twisted thinking can go.

God placed in each of us the need for affirmation, and we are called as a community to meet that need in one another. It strengthens our personal identity and significance.[15] In an environment of critique the need for affirmation isn't met, and so we start affirming ourselves.

It is sad, even pathetic, to hear people who need to promote themselves. Sometimes I have heard people critique another teacher or speaker and then pump themselves as if they are better. The Scripture tells us not to compare ourselves with others:

> Do we begin again to commend ourselves? Or do we need, as some others, epistles of commendation to you or letters of commendation from you? . . . And we have such trust through Christ toward God. Not that we are sufficient of ourselves to think of anything as being from ourselves, but our sufficiency is from God.
>
> 2 Corinthians 3:1, 4–5 NKJV

When someone brags, regardless of how sophisticated they are, it reveals an unmet need. An environment of grace meets that need, giving a person freedom to focus on others. When I am affirmed in who I am, I don't sit in meetings trying to posture myself to get noticed or to be considered worthy. I am released to minister to others, to focus on how I might help them live out God's dream for them. The happy result is that I can submit to others' strengths and protect their weaknesses.

15. Thrall and McNicol, *Forming the High-Trust Culture*, A-10.

Watching Each Other's Back

The United States Marine Corps has a code that they won't leave anyone behind. They recognize that each Marine has different strengths, and they watch each other's backs. They protect each other so there is limited exposure in battle. In an environment of grace we can relax and know that we will be protected—that our weaknesses will not be highlighted. This is particularly important to leaders who are often criticized.

As the leaders in our church built relationships of trust, we were able to watch each other's backs. I had been one of those task-oriented visionaries who can turn impatience into a virtue and deliberation into a sin. I see the big picture and then intuitively go for it. I believe in process and value its power to garner ownership of the group, but I definitely do not enjoy it. Yet sitting through decision-making meetings was the way I submitted to the strengths of the other leaders. My participation also showed them that I value how God made them and that I believe the product of this process will be better than if I had done it my way alone. In turn they protect me from the criticism that I am not interested in the opinions of others.

There must be a trust level before this can happen. I must trust that they won't critique my fidgeting and leaving the room more often than normal. They appreciate my strengths, and they realize that I will protect them from the criticism that they take too much time and lack faith because they want to analyze and plan. We believe in each other; we affirm how God has made each of us and thank him for it. We relish our differences and celebrate how it all works together in an environment of grace based on relationships of trust. People thrive in the safe confines of such a place.

Hitting a Sour Note

Even after my relationship with the elders improved, things did not immediately go smoothly with the congregation. We

decided to have visitor Sundays. We made flyers for the congregation to pass out to their friends and prepared a great, free meal
for all the guests. I told the congregation, "You are the outreach
program. We are residents in the harvest field, and now God
wants us to be transformed into workers in the harvest field."

The oddest thing happened—attendance went down on our
visitor Sundays. We were baffled; why would people stay away?
There were the normal thoughts: "They are weak and afraid."
"We are living in the last days; people don't care anymore." Of
course very few of the staff or elders brought anyone; I invited
my neighbors, but no one came.

I now believe I know why people stayed away. One major reason
was that most churchgoers don't have meaningful relationships
with unbelievers. But more importantly, the people perceived it as
a program to make the church bigger. We hadn't found the right
motivation; we were off-key and had hit a sour note.

The truth is that when we don't create the right relational
climate, it takes longer to accomplish the task. Relational
shortcuts don't work because we must turn around and start
again. It takes longer because you don't have the hearts of the
people. Remember, people only take in the truth that they
trust, and don't mistake information for truth that speaks to
the heart.

We had to retool and rethink our outreach plan because it had
to be about the passion of our church members to reach others.
And that is dependent on the environment in which they live.
If they are affirmed and accepted and trust those around them,
no one will be able to stop them from inviting others. Once they
are being transformed and fulfilled, they will want others they
love to experience it as well.

WHY OUR DISCIPLESHIP DOESN'T REPRODUCE

In chapter 2 I asserted that contemporary discipleship is
nonreproductive because we have lost what making disciples

meant in the first century. In particular, we do not practice the first and fifth characteristics of discipleship:

1. A disciple submits to a teacher who teaches him or her how to follow Jesus. That person provides accountability and, therefore, transformational traction.
5. A disciple finds and teaches other disciples for Jesus.

Those principles can be posted throughout the church, you can put bumper stickers on every car and mottoes on bulletins, T-shirts, and bracelets, but it won't happen unless people have relationships of trust.

This is a crucial issue that must be addressed honestly. *The environment of grace based on relationships of trust is the atmosphere in which transformation thrives.* People are more open to the truth of Scripture and change comes more easily when there is a high trust level. Once this happens, people will be more teachable, there will be a sweetness of cooperation, and people will be more willing to take risks because their acceptance is not based on performance.

A SWEET ENDING

I write these words five days after my last day as pastor of Cypress Church. The last five years have been a gift to me. God has reshaped my soul and given me a new message, and it would not have been possible outside that imperfect and growing community. Let me say again that character is built in community and is tested in isolation. I left Cypress Church because God used that community to reawaken my deepest calling. I am a discipleship evangelist, evangelizing the church worldwide to choose the life of discipleship.

It would never have occurred to me to take this step if I hadn't passed through the experience of the past five years. The day I submitted myself to them and said "I will trust you with me" was the day change began. I didn't run away; I climbed through the flames into the pain and emerged from it with a sweetness beyond my ability to describe.

I can recall the words I used to walk out into the light and risk revealing myself:

> Is it okay to let you know that I like the Eagles much more than Christian music? Is it okay that I find a lot of church activities just not me? That I think the *Left Behind* series is boring and the *Prayer of Jabez* overdone? Is it all right for me to tell you that I sometimes get angry and take it out on my wife, and on you? That sometimes my ambition gets the best of me, and I want to be treated with the honor my flesh thinks it deserves? That sometimes I see a beautiful woman and I spend a little too long looking at her? That I sometimes fear death, that there are moments when I doubt that Jesus is the only way and that there is a hell? Or that I should be a pastor, that I have spent twenty-five years of my life trying to be different so people will think I am worthy to be a pastor?

What I asked for that day was their acceptance. I told them they had mine: "There is nothing you could tell me about you that would cause me to love you any less." It became clear that I was getting through. Hundreds came to the altar to seek God and affirm their need for acceptance and their acceptance of me. I close this chapter with the words from the plaque the church gave me.

> Presented to Pastor Bill Hull:
> For years you have been a Christ-like example of zealous disciple-making, faithfulness, self-discipline, perseverance, commitment to excellence, willingness to humble yourself, devotion to living and teaching God's Word, prayerfulness, and self-sacrificing service. We "get it" that you love us.

They "got it" that I loved them, but only after I "got it" that loving as Christ loved was the essence of leadership.

8

SUBMISSION
AND THE LIFE

The one and only compelling reason for submission
is the example of Jesus.[1]

—Richard Foster

*S*ubmission is a word that raises the hair on most necks.
Submission—what religious extremists demand from their
wives and followers. *Submission*—what the religious and political
left deplores and will do anything to stop. It is what millions of

In reference to this chapter I again must acknowledge and express my gratitude to Bill
Thrall and Bruce McNicol. The idea that submission is a love word before it is an authority word is basic to their teaching. Other concepts that reflect the teaching of their
organization, Leadership Catalyst, are as follows: "living in light of who God says you
are," "submission is built on trust and integrity of relationships," "trusting others with
me," "the dynamics of relationships and trust," "relationships of trust and permission,"
"affirmation confirms our identity," "if we are not affirmed, we affirm ourselves," "affirmation never arouses sin," and "submitting to one another's strengths and protecting
each other's weaknesses." In addition, the continued references to environments of grace
and relationships of trust are integral to the teaching of Leadership Catalyst.

1. Richard Foster, *Celebration of Discipline* (San Francisco: Harper & Row, 1978), 102.

people fear will destroy their lives. Who in their right mind would submit to tyrannical governments and amoral corporations? Is it smart to let someone else run your life, to relinquish control, to limit your options? Isn't liberty life's greatest treasure; haven't many died in the pursuit of it or to protect it? Yes it is, and yes they have. Yet the greatest truth about submission is that we submit to what we trust. In the realm of political and religious leadership, integrity and trustworthiness are prerequisites for submission. The good news is that God doesn't require us to submit to governments or churches that violate our conscience. But we must be prepared to pay the consequences when we resist.

Resistance to authority runs much deeper than cultural experiences; it is hardwired into human personality. The most basic human trait is the desire to run our own lives, to maintain control in order to get what we want. You may have heard of the mother trying to control her seven-year-old at a restaurant. Johnny was running from table to table being cute, which brought great embarrassment to Mom. "Sit down, Johnny," she ordered. Johnny continued his little show, so in desperation Mom grabbed Johnny by the arm and sat him down in the booth. "Now you stay there in your seat." Johnny replied for all of us who hate being told what to do, "I may be sitting down on the outside, but I'm standing up on the inside." Often like Johnny we do comply, but only because we are out of options.

I would like to propose an understanding of submission that would make it our first option. Suppose I told you that submission is the door to liberty and the most empowering act of the human will? What if submission was understood as a love word before it becomes an authority word?

SUBMISSION: YOUR CREDENTIAL FOR TRANSFORMATION

Why an entire chapter on submission? Because until we understand its value, the following is true:

1. *We won't get our needs met*; therefore, we will live as needy people trying to fill the holes in our lives. All events, good or bad, will be all about us and what we need.
2. *We will lack humility*; therefore, God cannot bless us.
3. *We will shut out others from loving us*; therefore, we will live lives of isolation with an undeveloped character.

These three traits are part of the high cost of nondiscipleship. The example of Jesus shows us that what made it all work for him was his submission.

JESUS' CORE CHARACTER TRAIT

The essence is this: Jesus' core character trait was humility, which manifested itself in submission. If it does not become ours, then how can we believe that we are being transformed into his image? This is the heart of Jesus' life and mission; everything else flows from it. There is no way to read Paul's teaching on this subject and draw any other conclusion.

Let this mind be in you which was also in Christ Jesus, who, being in the form of God, did not consider it robbery to be equal with God, but made Himself of no reputation, *taking the form of a servant*, and coming in the likeness of men. And being found in appearance as a man, He humbled Himself and became obedient to the point of death, even the death of the cross.

Philippians 2:5–8 NKJV, emphasis added

I am attracted to radical, but this is so radical even I don't like it. I am a marginal iconoclast, but I enjoy breaking more than being broken. Brokenness before God means to relinquish all rights and dreams, to submit them to God's greater good and purpose. This passage reminds me of Henri Nouwen's words that following Jesus means resisting the temptation to be relevant. He wrote, "I am deeply convinced that the Christian leader of the future is called to be completely irrelevant and to stand in this world with nothing to offer but his or her own vulnerable self."[2] Some might want to dismiss Nouwen as a brilliant nonconformist whose monkish tendencies created such an impractical statement. But it could be that irrelevancy is the road to world impact.

The gurus of the inner life have been preaching at us for hundreds of years: slow down, be quiet, kill the monster within that insists on being first, being noticed, being praised, that can be found preening itself atop achievement. Many have written them off as necessary reminders of an ancient life of contemplation and peace locked away behind the thick walls of retreat centers. The prevailing evangelical mind says what we need are soldiers charging into the battle mounted on the engine of technology, armed with strategic plans and procedures. Could it be that we have been terribly wrong? Have we ignored Jesus as our Leader and chosen lesser gods? It very well could be that we should drop our laptops and palm pilots and reconsider.

Earlier chapters have documented our ineptness. We are well-meaning but ineffective in reaching the world around us. We might be able to dismiss the impracticality of the desert fathers and Benedictines, but we can't dismiss Jesus as irrelevant. He is the one we are to become like, to follow, to learn from, and to imitate in character, methods, and every way we can identify. Let's explore what Jesus' example means.

LET THIS MIND BE IN YOU

"Let this mind be in you which was also in Christ Jesus" (Phil. 2:5 NKJV). Instead of "mind," many translations say "attitude" from *phronos*, meaning "mind-set" or "frame of mind" (for example, NIV, NASB). It is written in the imperative, so it isn't a

2. Henri J. M. Nouwen, *In the Name of Jesus: Reflections on Christian Leadership* (New York: Crossroad, 1989), 17.

suggestion. The attitude that Jesus models for us is, therefore, necessary to any relevancy in mission.

What we find at the very heart of this mind-set are the words, "did not consider equality with God something to be grasped" (Phil. 2:6). What torments most of us is that we are not considered equal to others with whom we work or to those whose homes are a little closer to the beach, higher on the hill, or near the seventh green. How about those whose cars are shinier, faster, and bigger? But being equal isn't enough for us; down deep we want to be considered superior. I live six blocks from the beach, and sometimes a little shot of pleasure goes through me when people walk by as they leave the beach because I know they live farther away from the water than I do. Smugness is written on the faces of first-class passengers as the coach passengers file on after they are already seated and sipping their drinks. Our hands are extended and open as we strain forward to grab hold of the immediate pleasures offered us. But the radical nature of thinking like Jesus is not to care about the things for which everyone else is grasping. This passage not only speaks of the obvious worldly booty but also the false promise of fame, recognition, and praise from others. Jesus didn't consider it valuable; he saw through it; he saw it all as a fine meal that satisfies only for a short period.

The word *consider* means to hold an opinion; it reflects a person's worldview. In order to counteract the grasping for advantage and recognition, there must exist a counterforce. That counterforce is the life of Jesus in us. But we must do more than have him live in us; we must adopt his mind through prayer and the practice of the disciplines Jesus modeled. Most of us will need help in community to walk with others who have the same goal. Frankly, this is so countercultural you will need to be careful in choosing with whom you walk (Luke 6:39–40). Jesus rejected the life of other religious leaders; in fact he did so with a stinging rebuke:

> Do not do what they do, for they do not practice what they preach.
> They tie up heavy loads and put them on other men's shoulders,

but they themselves are not willing to lift a finger to move them. Everything they do is done for men to see: . . . they love the place of honor . . . they love to be greeted in the marketplaces and to have men call them "Rabbi."

Matthew 23:2–7

When I read this rebuke I can't help but see myself in the description. We love to be called "doctor," "author," "nationally known speaker," "dynamic leader." We love to be the headliner at major conferences and be ranked among the Who's Who of great leaders of the past century. The pull is so strong on high achievers because it has two powerful sources—the flesh on the inside and the praise of culture on the outside. And there are many rewards—the development of a public identity that satisfies the ego and very often financial success and all its trappings. Just remember what Rodin Scott says, "When our daily self-worth and the measure of our effectiveness come primarily from the reaction of those with whom we work, then we are finished as Christian leaders."[3]

JESUS DID NOT TRUST THE WORLD'S TRUTH

Jesus didn't go along with the world's truth because he recognized the false promises. Instead he chose to be irrelevant to that value system and in doing so became the most relevant person in history. With a little prying we can find what he trusted and why. He didn't trust the heart of man: "Many people saw the miraculous signs he was doing and believed in his name. But Jesus would not entrust himself to them, for he knew all men . . . for he knew what was in a man" (John 2:23–25).

The cross is proof enough that Jesus was totally committed to people. But he didn't entrust himself to them because he had a perfect understanding of the fickleness of humans (Jer. 17:9). One of the plainest facts of history is that Jesus didn't trust the

---

3. R. Rodin Scott, *Becoming a Leader of No Reputation* (unpublished paper).

Sanhedrin or the Roman courts. What Jesus did trust was the truth and promises that came from his Father.

> Jesus gave them this answer. "I tell you the truth, the Son can do nothing by himself; he can do only what he sees his Father doing, because whatever the Father does the Son also does. For the Father loves the Son and shows him all he does."
>
> John 5:19–20

Only this kind of confidence can cause a person to forsake the world's relevancy.

Paul said that Jesus "humbled himself and became obedient to death—even death on a cross!" (Phil. 2:8). Humility requires comparison and obedience requires a greater authority. For Jesus it was submission to his Father that gave him the capacity to go it alone, to walk against the prevailing winds of time and culture. As followers of Jesus, our humility is based on a comparison with our Leader and our obedience is to his authority in our lives. His example, sacrifice, and person are enough for us to trust, enabling us to commit to his way.

JESUS MADE HIMSELF OF NO REPUTATION

Philippians 2:7 (NKJV) does not say "bad or notorious reputation"; it says "no reputation." Now everyone has a reputation, so this doesn't mean that no one had any opinion about Jesus. We know that Jesus was famous in his time; he had thousands of admirers and hundreds of followers. This has more to do with his mind-set than those around him. He lived based on his own view of who he was, who his Father said he was: "This is My beloved Son, in whom I am well pleased" (Matt. 3:17 NKJV). The trust of their relationship overpowered every other opinion and force. It won over who the multitudes of people following him thought Jesus was, over who his disciples said he was, and over who the religious establishment said Jesus was. They considered him a healer, a marvelous teacher, a worker of miracles, a maverick, and/or a blasphemer. Jesus saw himself as a servant:

> You know that the rulers of the Gentiles lord it over them, and those who are great exercise authority over them. Yet it shall not be so among you; but whoever desires to become great among you, let him be your servant. And whoever desires to be first among you, let him be your slave—just as the Son of Man did not come to be served, but to serve, and to give His life a ransom for many.
>
> Matthew 20:25–28

How many of us are driven to serve, to sacrifice our rights and privileges? Jesus was committed to a different kind of greatness—a greatness that slays the power that reputation holds over us. Richard Foster said,

> The most radical social teaching of Jesus was His total reversal of the contemporary notion of greatness. Leadership is found in becoming the servant of all. Power is discovered in submission. The foremost symbol of this radical servanthood is the cross. . . . He flatly rejected the cultural givens of position and power when he said "you are not to be called Rabbi . . . neither called masters." He took women seriously and was willing to meet with children, he took the towel and washed his disciples' feet.[4]

Pride can be our greatest obstacle to following Jesus' example of servanthood. I once held a prestigious position with my denomination in which I was charged with oversight of the national ministries. I had accepted the position with the understanding that I would be the denominational president's "go to guy" and work closely with him. After a few years the suggestion came up that I should report to the executive vice president, a newly created position. I really liked the executive vice president and found him easy to work with, but I rejected the idea because it

4. Foster, *Celebration of Discipline*, 101.

meant I would be watched more closely and be one step removed from the president. It also made me look a little less important in the organization.

I told the president that I didn't want to make this change, and I thought because of my cachet with the leaders, they would not force anything down my throat. However, I found out at a breakfast meeting that I had been wrong. I was informed that the decision had already been made by the board of directors without any direct input from me. I was very angry, not so much that I would be reporting to the executive vice president but that I was treated as a mere employee. My cachet had crashed; I hadn't been treated with the respect and deference I felt I deserved.

Pride is an evil thing. They had taken my pride and stuffed it down my throat, and I didn't like the taste. I was stewing in my anger and self-pity when God reminded me of these words that Jesus "made Himself of no reputation. . . . He humbled Himself and became obedient to . . . death" (Phil. 2:7–8 NKJV). C. S. Lewis said pride is essentially competitive: "Pride gets no pleasure of having something, only out of having more of it than the next man."[5] In the depths of my soul my pride didn't want to submit; I wanted to have it my way. I wanted others to say, "Bill, you are so talented and valuable to us that we wouldn't want to do anything to disturb your motivation and genius."

The next day I was asked to give a short devotional thought to the annual conference. It was easy. I spoke on the power of fitting in, the power of submission as the doorway to God's kind of greatness.

The model and message of Jesus is that submission is the greatest force on the earth. He submitted to his Father, the world's sins were paid for, we submit to him, and that same power radiates out from us to others. The daily challenge of following Jesus is living in the truth of who he says we are and in the light of his definition of greatness, which is service. In the

5. C. S. Lewis, *Mere Christianity*, in *A Guide to Prayer for Ministers and Other Servants*, comp. Rueben P. Job and Norman Shawchuck (Nashville: Upper Room, 1983), 126.

end the rewards are as he promised, "Whoever loses his life for me will save it" (Luke 9:24).

JESUS HUMBLED HIMSELF AND BECAME OBEDIENT

Jesus' humility was based on who his Father said he was, not on who others said he was. When I was angry over not being treated as I thought I deserved, I was working from a false identity—a fragile identity that depended on how I was treated and what others around me thought of me. This is the way of the proud and high-strung. If Jesus had followed this method, his mission would have failed. Instead he accepted an appearance that was the understatement of history. One can only imagine the slights of those who didn't realize how deeply they needed him, the cold stares of others for whom he was prepared to die. It is outside my comprehension to grasp the depth of that kind of love. It is one thing to return good for evil in the mundane of life. But a love that will take the rejection when you don't have to—that requires more than our admiration; it must have our worship. He was in his very nature a servant.

When you have the rock solid identity that you are loved and valued by God, you can take on any role and be satisfied because a pleased God will do what is best for his child. I appeared to be less powerful in my demotion, but in fact I was more powerful. Once I saw my pride and repented, my character had more force, more ability to penetrate others.

Have you ever noticed how much more powerful it is when people lead with humility? Humility has a razor edge that can cut through virtually every resistance to truth. Malcolm Muggeridge stated this powerfully in his description of Mother Teresa:

> She is a nun, rather slightly built, with a few rupees in her pocket; not particularly clever or particularly gifted in the arts of persuasion. Just with this Christian love shining about her; in her

heart and on her lips. Just prepared to follow her Lord. And in accordance with his instructions regard every derelict left to die in the streets as him; to hear in the cry of every abandoned child, even in the tiny squeak of the discarded fetus, the cry of the Bethlehem child; to recognize in every leper's stumps the hands which once touched sightless eyes and made them see, rested on distracted heads and made them calm, brought back health to sick flesh and twisted limbs. As for my expatiations on Bengal's wretched social conditions—I regret to say that I doubt whether, in any divine accounting, they will equal one single quizzical half smile bestowed by Mother Teresa on a street urchin who happened to catch her eye.[6]

The power of humility is seen in the way it serves. It does what many won't; it gives rather than takes. Submission to mission is the cornerstone of humility, of living in the light of who God says we are. Laying aside our culturally driven dreams and submitting to his vision for us guides our feet to walk in the good works that he prepared beforehand (Eph. 2:10). Paul encourages us to find ways of living out the power of humility and submission.

> Therefore, my dear friends, as you have always obeyed—not only in my presence, but now much more in my absence—continue to *work out your salvation* with fear and trembling, for it is God who works in you *to will* and *to act* according to his good purpose.
>
> Philippians 2:12–13, emphasis added

This is really what it means to follow Jesus: to work out what God works in us. God works in us *to will*—that means that he puts his desires in us. How does one distinguish the culturally driven dreams from God's impulses? Jesus is our guide. His greatest value was to submit to his Father because their hearts were connected. Jesus lived in light of who his Father said he was. This is the same as our living in light of who God says we are rather than what the surrounding world says we are. The culture

6. Malcolm Muggeridge, *Something Beautiful for God*, in *A Guide to Prayer*, 111.

defines us by looks, pedigree, and achievement; God says we are his children with an eternal inheritance and specific purpose that he has prepared for us.

People in this frame of mind will listen for God's voice. They are humble and committed enough to lay aside all other agendas in order to find God's. They have chosen the life; they are willing to become servants, to live lives of sacrifice. In this frame of mind the impulses of God are recognized and we begin to act, to obey the desires he plants in us. This is not static; it is a dynamic and daily experience.

I recently had lunch with a friend who is listening to God's voice very well. He went to the altar at an evening service and while there God told him to contact two people. It didn't make that much sense because one person had been mad at him and the other he would see in just a few minutes. Why should he call them on his cell phone on the way home? But he obeyed God's direction.

The first was a man who was mad at him because he had confronted him about sin in his life. He called and caught the man sitting in front of the fireplace pondering his life. When my friend told him that God had prompted him to call and tell him how much he loved him, the man broke into tears. It was a powerful touch from God. Then he called his daughter, who he was to see in a few minutes. He found that she was about to leave his house and he would have missed her. He just wanted to tell her what a great daughter and mother she was. It was a touching moment, and again another person was ministered to because a humble servant was available to hear God's voice and reach out. He worked out what God had worked in him.

SUBMISSION AND THE COMMUNITY OF CHRIST

Jesus' core character trait was humility, which led to submission, which led to obedience, which led to the cross, which led to the rescue of humanity from the death grip of sin. *Submission* is a love word because it was based on the relationship between Jesus and his Father. Jesus considered his Father trustworthy and, therefore, submission was possible. So the core character trait of the disciple is also *humility before God and a life of submission based on who God says we are.* To choose the life means to choose humility and submission. It is the doorway to power and impact because it is being what Jesus was and doing what Jesus did.

A Spirit-filled community is a culture of willing submission—it is what Spirit-filled people do (Eph. 5:21). There are a few very clear, indisputable truths in the Scripture. One of them is that Spirit-filled people speak in positive, grace-filled ways to others. They have a deep, abiding joy inside and a heart of thanksgiving. And they are submissive to one another based on reverence for Christ (Eph. 5:15–21). The opposite is just as true: Critical people are those without joy and contentment who are resistant to authority in their lives and are not filled with the Spirit.

Submission is a choice to follow and be like Jesus. We voluntarily submit to the Lord by faith as an act of obedience because we trust in God's truth. We do so from the heart because we believe in God's love and goodness and are convinced that the plan he has developed for us is better and more affirming than our own plans. Here are some examples of how we are to submit:

All disciples are to submit to one another (Eph. 5:21).

Wives are to submit to husbands (Eph. 5:22).

Employees are to submit to employers (Eph. 6:5).

Followers are to submit to teachers (1 Thess. 5:12).

Followers are to submit to church leaders (Heb. 13:17).

Christians are to submit to the government (Rom. 13:1).

When It Gets Tough

Relationships can be—no, relationships *are* difficult. And submission becomes a gut-wrenching battle between our Lord's command and our wills, even our common sense. The wife wonders why she should submit to a husband who isn't qualified to lead her. The unfairly treated employee, student, or parishioner can find strong reasons to resist. There are many good articles and books that deal with special circumstances and where to draw the line. The general principle is that when you are asked to disobey God or violate your conscience, you are released from the call to submit. There is a price to pay when this happens, and God does not always immediately move in to solve the problem. He seems more interested in building our character and using it to influence those around us than changing our circumstances. But I thank God for every time he does change a negative circumstance.

When Everybody Disappears

"He humbled himself and became obedient to death—even death on a cross!" (Phil. 2:8). The calling to submit is not revoked when our assignment gets tough. Jesus models for us what happens when our support structures are stripped away. He took up his cross and was prepared to submit to his Father regardless of how difficult it became. Even his disciples abandoned him; all he had left was his Father. In his agony in Gethsemane, Jesus took up the difficulty of his assignment with his Father. Three times he asked to be let out, and each time the answer was *no*.

Submission is normal in a Spirit-filled culture, but even in that environment of grace it can be difficult. Submission is built on trust and the integrity of relationships. If we want to go deeper with God, others in the community must be involved. In chapter 2 it was established that the first step in spiritual formation is submitting to another person who can teach us how to follow Jesus—a spiritual director and friend who can walk with us on the journey. We need this because until we unmask ourselves in an environment of grace in a relationship of trust, we can't deal with the real self.

When the people we have depended on are not there anymore, will God be enough? This is what reveals our motive. Were we in submission for the approval of our boss, teacher, pastor, or spouse? What about another person or two who have walked with us; did we stay at it because of them? The answer has to be *yes*; relationships have to be the reason we do many things. But the lesson from Jesus is that when our support system is gone, our relationship with God himself should be sufficient to motivate and sustain our staying in the mission.

Staying the Course

Jane and I are very close to a family who are church planting in Cambodia. Dave and Lisa Everritt got married while attending the church I was pastoring. Dave was an outstanding pastor on our staff and touched people in a very special way. He and Lisa sensed a call to serve and work among the poor. They moved to Cambodia eight years ago. Dave has an unusual gift of compassion, and he is able to relate to people more powerfully than any person I know.

A couple of years into their first term, Dave got sick. In fact he went through a series of illnesses that depleted him both physically and emotionally. They had to return to the States for rest and refreshing. While back home, their son Malachi started having problems with his sight. For a short time he was blind. It was a gracious gift that a doctor familiar with tropical diseases was able to diagnose Malachi as having a parasite in his brain. He was treated and returned to normal.

The difficulty of Dave getting well and the experience with Malachi would have caused many people to retreat from submission to their call. Then Lisa began to have horrible headaches and was rushed to the hospital. After several agonizing days of tests and pain, the diagnosis was a growth or tumor in Lisa's brain. It looked like the Everritts would need to stay home and not return to Cambodia. But they never gave in and began to seek God's healing for Lisa. Weeks went by and Lisa underwent treatment, but it didn't seem to be working. Many people were praying for Lisa, and a fellow elder and I joined another pastor one morning and anointed Lisa with oil and prayed for her healing. Within a few days the growth disappeared.

After all this and against the advice of many, the Everritts returned to Cambodia three years ago. Dave works in an Army hospital with AIDS patients. The life cycle from entry into the hospital to death is three years. In Dave's church, you choose Christ the first year, become a leader the second year, and then die the third year. He also uses his prodigious motorcycle skills to travel the back roads of Cambodia to preach, teach, and train pastors. One of Dave's ministries is teaching Cambodian pastors to ride a motorcycle in rough terrain.

Recently Lisa has experienced some seizures, but the tests show nothing, and they are staying the course. The temptation to do something else can be strong at times, but they are being obedient even through sickness and trials. Dave and Lisa have tapped into what Jesus modeled and what saw him through in staying on mission. Their submission to the Father is the basis for their commitment.

This is about whom you trust. God gives us a support system, but in the end, you stay the course because he himself is enough. It is about his love and goodness, that there is no better life than the one God has planned. That is how you know you are well off, that you are living the good life. Dave and Lisa are living the good life in Cambodia.

LIVING A SUBMISSIVE LIFE

I mentioned earlier that a life of individualism and independence will create three realities that will make it impossible for transformation:

1. We won't get our needs met.
2. We will lack humility.
3. We will shut out others from loving us.

Conversely the submissive life will lead to having our needs met, developing humility, and giving others permission to love us.

Our Needs Are Met

Every person needs affirmation, and without it some ugly things happen. Affirmation confirms our identity and appreciates our strengths and contributions.[7] It brings us out of our shells and makes us more willing to take risks.

If we are not affirmed, we will begin to affirm ourselves. If no one pays any attention to us, we will start doing things to get others to notice us. The obvious examples are the blowhard at a party or the teenager with spiked orange hair and a ring attached to some delicate part of the anatomy. And of course there is the classic name-dropper, "I had breakfast with President Bush last Thursday" (failing to add that it was at the National Prayer Breakfast with four thousand others and he was seventy-five yards away from the president but could see him on the big screen).

Have you ever sat in a meeting for hours, even days, without being noticed, and when you do speak it doesn't go anywhere? How does it feel? You become anxious; you start looking for opportunities to score a point that will bolster that sinking feeling of insignificance. You may even write down points on which you can argue, since winning an argument would make them respect you. This is sad because if you knew that the group fully accepted and respected you, you could relax and be yourself. This scenario also reveals our pathological dependence on others for self-identity.

What if that group meeting had started with an exercise of affirmation that reinforced your gifts and how others felt about your contribution to their lives? That would have created a safe environment in which you could have relaxed and made a genuine contribution that wouldn't have risen out of a crisis of unmet need.

7. Bill Thrall and Bruce McNicol, *Forming the High-Trust Culture* (Leadership Catalyst, 2000), A-10.

If anyone needed affirmation and reinforcement of his gifts, it was Timothy. How would you like following the apostle Paul as pastor of the church at Ephesus? Following a hardworking, talented person is tough enough, but an apostle as well! Timothy was younger, shy, known to have a nervous tummy, and easily intimidated (1 Tim. 4:11–16; 2 Tim. 1:7–8; 2:1; 4:1–4). He was being hammered by the various opinions of who he was in comparison to Paul and how he should conduct his work as pastor.

Paul is considered by many a tough taskmaster and possibly not very tuned in to emotional needs. I find that opinion to be an almost laughable caricature of a highly passionate man who loved and hated with great force. Instead I believe Paul was very sensitive to what people were feeling. Someone so in touch with his own emotions would have a high emotional intelligence. He sensed Timothy's need and began his second letter to Timothy with a powerful affirmation (2 Tim. 1:3–7):

> I thank God for you.
> I pray for you night and day.
> I think about you all the time.
> I remember your tears.
> I long to see you.
> I am filled with joy when I am around you.

What kind of effect does this affirmation have on a person? I suggested to our congregation that if every husband went home and said this to his wife or child, it could transform their relationship. One man did exactly that. He is a Christian and his wife is not, so he thought he would try out these affirmations on her. She broke into tears and gave him a tremendous hug.

Affirmation is powerful, and it is better than critique because it actually creates an environment that gives people permission to drop their defenses. As a result, deep changes can take place. I have never known affirmation to arouse sin. When I receive praise, I am humbled that God would send one of his children to affirm me. It is for that reason that I am aroused to a higher effort.

We Will Develop Humility

Submission is an act of humility based on our belief in God's love and goodness. Submission is choosing to let God meet our needs. We cannot experience love without submission, and without submission we lack humility. Without humility, God's grace is closed off from our lives (1 Peter 5:5).

Humility comes from the Latin word *humus*, meaning "fertile ground." It is the fertile soil ready to receive the seed of God's Word. It accepts its low place and is ready to be used as a way for God to express himself. Evelyn Underhill wrote that "we mostly spend our lives conjugating three verbs: to want, to have and to do. Craving, clutching, and fussing. . . . they only have meaning in so far as they are transcended by and included in, the fundamental verb to be: and being, not wanting, having and doing, is the essence of a spiritual life."[8]

Humility was Jesus' core characteristic; he modeled life in submission with a greater purpose. To follow him requires the same humility, the same willingness to be like fertile soil for the use of the Father. He will grow his life in us, and we will find joy in giving and serving. As we do so, God will bless us.

Protecting Weakness

Humility leads to submission, and submission creates even more humility. As we humbly allow others to speak into our lives, their strengths will protect us from our weaknesses. The more we experience other people's love and help, the more we will desire it.

Paul had Timothy's permission to speak into his life, which gave us the letters to Timothy. Paul was strong where Timothy was weak, so Paul told him to stay strong, to teach faithfully, to stick with his gifts, to not allow others to look down on his youth. The classic statement is, "Hence I remind you to rekindle

8. Evelyn Underhill, *The Spiritual Life*, in *A Guide to Prayer*, 320.

the gift of God that is within you through the laying on of my hands; for God did not give us a spirit of timidity but a spirit of power and love and self-control" (2 Tim. 1:6–7).

Paul very strongly recalled Timothy's commission, with which Timothy was apparently struggling due to the difficulties of pastoral ministry. The New International Version translates it "fan into flame the gift of God" that was in him. The picture is one of dying embers in need of oxygen. Timothy was obviously off course, fearful, caving in to pressure on a number of fronts, questioning his call, and sitting up at night with an upset stomach. The relationship of trust was there—Timothy didn't have any doubt regarding Paul's love and commitment to him. For that reason he could humble himself and submit, especially to Paul's strengths. Therefore, Paul was able to speak directly into his life, which allowed Paul to love Timothy through his gifts and abilities.

This also brought protection to Timothy. The church leaders and members at Ephesus were in possession of the Ephesian letter, which presented the role of pastors and teachers as well as the role members were to play in the church environment (Eph. 4:11–16). Those who were pressuring Timothy were also able to read Paul's letter to him. Can you imagine Timothy being able to keep such a treasure a secret from the leaders or for that matter from the congregation at large? The letters to Timothy then protected him from the wolves that sought to devour him.

Protecting one another is an undeveloped skill in too many of our faith communities. "George is a nice guy with a good heart but. . . ." This is the kind of protection we give, and it isn't good enough. What comes after the *but* is what causes George to retreat to the safe confines of the hidden life.

Humble people who are willing to submit to one another's strengths can learn to truly love and protect each other. We can be trained to think of others as gifts from God who can contribute based on how God has made and called them without requiring them to be good at many other things. In fact we might learn to say, "George is really good at organization, and we thank God for him. We don't expect him to lead or understand much about counseling or small groups. That is the way we treat each other around here. We all do what we can do and don't expect more than God does out of any person. We find people who are called and gifted for those other areas and celebrate that they can do that."

What We Want in Relationships

One can only imagine the way Paul and Timothy got to this level of communication. You may remember that Paul told the Corinthians that he would send Timothy to them to take care of matters. Paul called him a "son in the Lord" and said, "He will remind you of my ways in Christ" (1 Cor. 4:17 NKJV). From the very first time they met outside of Timothy's hometown of Lystra until the end of Paul's life, they were close. Paul had great confidence in Timothy. There was no mission he would not trust him with—even the dangerous work with the fickle Corinthians. I am sure that Timothy was able to minister to Paul and speak into his life as well.

Could you imagine the power of our discipleship if we could relate in such an environment of acceptance and affirmation? Paul and Timothy submitted to each other's strengths and protected each other's weaknesses. This takes place when we drop our guard and become open and honest with each other. Once we accept that it is okay for each of us to be the person God made us to be and that we don't have to have it all working right, then we can help each other keep our commitments to God.

Jesus Emptied Himself

Jesus' core character trait was his humility and submission to his Father's agenda. The text says he "emptied himself" (Phil. 2:7 RSV). *Emptied* is from *ekenosen*, "to completely remove or eliminate elements of high status or rank by eliminating all privileges or prerogatives associated with such status or rank—to empty oneself, to divest oneself of position."[9] That means Jesus took the shape (*morphen*) of a slave (*doulou*). There is great mystery surrounding such a choice regarding the composition of the God-man. What we do know is that Jesus willed it; he made a choice to change his earthly posture that was rooted in his love for and trust in the Father's perfect goodness. Jesus found that sufficient for his humility and submission. The challenge for us is to believe in the love of the Father and then trust our Leader Jesus as we commit to transformation starting where he did, with humility and submission.

9. Eugene Peterson and Marva Dawn, *The Unnecessary Pastor* (Grand Rapids: Eerdmans, 2000), 141.

9

LEADERSHIP
AND THE LIFE

The Church or something like it must be cherished,
criticized, nourished and reformed. The Church of
Jesus Christ, with all its blemishes, its divisions and
its failures, remains our best hope of spiritual vitality.
However poor it is, life without it is worse.[1]

—Elton Trueblood

I don't think the church will ever live up to our idyllic theories.
It struggles because we, its members, struggle. It is broken
because we, the participants, are broken. It will always in one
way or another be in crisis until we are completely transformed
into Christ's likeness (1 John 3:1).

1. Elton Trueblood, *The Company of the Committed*, in James R. Newby, *The Best of Elton Trueblood* (Nashville: Impact Books, 1979), 26.

There is a myth afoot that says as I grow spiritually I become less needy and less dependent, and after a certain discipleship regime I will have it together. Discipleship is a lifelong process, and I will be extremely needy until that wonderful moment I am completely and eternally changed. In fact the more I become like Jesus, the more I am dependent on him.

What I am saying is that the church will always vacillate between glory and the grotesque. *Grotesque* is defined as, "Characterized by distortions or striking incongruities in appearance, shape, manner; fantastic or bizarre . . . strange, eccentric, ridiculous and absurd."[2] I think I use *grotesque* quite accurately. But then there is the glory and the stunning fact that there is nothing else. But as Trueblood says, the church is our best hope for spiritual vitality, and "however poor it is, life without it is worse." Now this seems to be an odd admission considering that the previous chapters have called upon the reader to raise the bar of what is considered the normal Christian life. Yes, we will always struggle, but there will be periods of great glory when Christ is paramount and the world all around will be infected with the life of Christ through us.

There are moments when the glory of Christ is the dominant characteristic of the church. The glory is when our little communities of grace show those around us who God is and what God has. It is for these periods of glory that we live, for which we train, and for which we pray.

Whenever Elton Trueblood drove by a church, especially a small rural one, he would tip his hat, for there inside that little wooden building with a steeple was the best hope of humankind. So who will plunge headfirst and lead this community of both the grotesque and the glorious? It is to you, the company of the committed,[3] that I now write in the remainder of this chapter.

2. *Webster's New World Dictionary*, 2d ed., s.v. "grotesque."
3. Term borrowed from Elton Trueblood, *The Company of the Committed* (San Francisco: Harper & Row, 1961). Trueblood's book names those who are willing to choose the life and commit to a life of sacrifice and service to Christ.

THE PASTORAL CONDITION

As a boy I arose early on Saturdays so I could get my chores done so I could watch my favorite program, *The Three Stooges*. Even today I laugh out loud when I catch a few minutes of their slapstick antics. Most kids my age knew all the moves, phrases, and characters. There were a total of five stooges over the years, but my favorite trio was Larry, Moe, and Curley. And Curley was my man; he made it all work for me. Without debate, the number one line I remember was Curley calling out in panic "Moe, Larry . . . CHEESE." It would always be a moment of personal crisis for Curley, usually when he was about to lose control and hurt someone. So Moe and Larry would rush to get Curley some cheese; they would stuff it in his mouth and Curley would magically become calm. Cheese was what Curley needed and once that need was met he would be fine until the next crisis.

THE TRAP

I would like to use cheese as a metaphor for what culture offers the spiritual leader to quiet our manic need for adulation and acceptance. It seems that many leaders are just as frantic about needing their cheese as Curley. I know that I have been and I couldn't feel good about life unless I was getting my ego needs met regularly. How many accolades was I getting about my messages, books, and leadership? Where was I invited to speak and by whom and before how many? This is all part of the cheese, the needs that must be met. It is the delectable morsel that is readily available and quick to satisfy. I see it like a trap set for an animal that enters the cage to get its needs met and suddenly the door slams behind it and there it is, a prisoner. That trap is the prevailing pattern for pastoral leadership.

We find ourselves trapped in a world that rewards numerical and financial success. This mind-set is just as real in the church world as any. So we try and be successful by working to grow a church. If we grow a big one, then there is plenty of cheese. If not, we are trapped in the cage but without cheese. We read books and go to conferences where the "big cheese" leaders talk about their success. We return home and try out their methods and programs and guess what? They don't work the same. And then we find ourselves trapped in this system where recognition is supreme. Oscar Wilde once said "there are two tragedies in life, one is not getting what you want, and the other is getting it."

Those who are trapped in the American church system of rewards and punishments strive to do what works in order to build a career, climb the ecclesiastical ladder, and get the recognition and feedback needed to build a desired image. This does not mean it is evil to have a good career or any of the attributes above. What it does mean, however, is that many will fail by these standards and will be punished by a lack of rewards such as higher salaries, larger churches, and recognition among their peers. It is tragic when a person is trapped in a system in which he or she is moderately successful and largely unrewarded. As one sage put it, "There is nothing as sad as a man who is mediocre at what he loves." And the church has told him or her by what it honors and ignores that he or she is average, mediocre, regular, not one of the elite.

It is a tragedy when someone is made to feel mediocre, and it is just as tragic that church culture behaves this way and that too many leaders go along with it. The other tragedy, however, is those who do succeed, because they are trapped in the same system that is temporarily working for them. They become addicted to the same superficial reward system, which will eventually run out and leave them desperate.

Regardless of where you are on the American church food chain, you need to escape the tyranny of superficial goals and rewards. How does one escape? Successful leaders by contemporary standards can be just as miserable as those who are failing because they have all their identity needs met but now realize how empty it all is. So many thought there were rich rewards to be found in success measured in fame, recognition from peers, and the praise of the masses only to find it vacuous and unable to satisfy the hunger of the soul.

Is there a better way, a different way of being that satisfies for the long term? Is there a way of living and following Jesus that will open a new door to a deeper and stronger life? I want to scream, *"Yes, yes, yes!"* I say this because our Leader, Jesus, showed us how. To understand our Leader's life is to understand that greatness is something far different than what the world, especially the church world, offers.

GET OUT OF THE TRAP

Get out now while the door is open; go in search of a new way of spiritual sustenance. Change what makes you go, tick, work, or feel satisfied, and redefine what gives you joy. Leave behind the short-term rewards of adulation and reputation and choose the life of discipleship.

What an odd, even insulting thing for me to say to you, the company of the committed. "Discipleship?" you might protest, "Hey, man, that is what I am doing; that is my life." Is it really? Who are you following? Is it the Jesus who took a pass on adulation and reputation, who suffered and served, who was rejected, and who failed in the eyes of most (Phil. 2:5–8)? Do you follow the Jesus who rejected any shortcuts offered to him by the culture, even the religious culture, the Jesus who only looked to his Father for applause and direction?

Dietrich Bonhoeffer described the essence of discipleship, "It is nothing else than bondage to Jesus Christ alone, completely breaking through every program, every ideal, every set of laws. No other significance is possible, since Jesus is the only significance. Beside Jesus nothing has any significance. He alone matters."[4]

Isn't it true that many of us have followed a theological school of thought or system? It is undeniable that some leaders are of

4. Dietrich Bonhoeffer, *The Cost of Discipleship* (1937; reprint, New York: Macmillan and Company, 1963), 63.

the Reformed stream, others a modified dispensational, and still others charismatic. Each school of thought comes with accoutrements such as modes of worship and preaching. So we find ourselves in pursuit of how Jesus has led others of our tradition—other people in different settings, with different skills, team chemistry, and set of circumstances.

There are schools of thought with regard to philosophy of ministry. Some may adhere to some plan learned from a successful ministry or leader. Of course following Jesus is embedded in the various approaches, but it is not central with regard to method of ministry, means of reaching others, and what is valued. Almost all provide proof that they work by an increase in size.

What I am talking about, however, is an old way that is new to me and many like me. It is Jesus' way of being and doing—a way that I believe will change leaders and then the church and finally society. This journey begins with the personal choice of the leader who must ask, Who will I follow? What kind of life do I choose? If you do choose this kind of life, the following thoughts may provide direction.

COMMIT TO BE IRRELEVANT AND UNNECESSARY

Moving my source of sustenance means the source of my motivation has changed. It means I am no longer trapped in the fickle world of performance and results. God loves me—I mean he really loves me like a caring Father. He believes in me and will not lose faith or confidence in who I am and his dream for me (Eph. 2:10). Therefore, I can trust his leadership for me. He cares for me more than I do myself, and his plan is good and perfect for me. So I can take the frightening step toward what some would call oblivion but what Jesus calls freedom.

So let's begin by returning to the words of Henri Nouwen: "I am deeply convinced that the Christian leader of the future is called to be completely irrelevant and to stand in this world with nothing to offer but his or her own vulnerable self."[5] This means to lead with your weakness. We have been told to always lead with our résumé—the sanitized and enhanced version of ourselves. For instance, my résumé or biographical sketch tells my life's mission, the books I have written, the positions I have held, and the dreams I hold dear. Historically it was common to include a statement such as, "and is in constant demand as a speaker and advisor." This always makes me cringe, and thankfully it is on its way out. But for years it was an important part of résumé style, which I feel points to our need to be identified as important, relevant, wise, with a lot to offer.

You might remember when President Bill Clinton was stung by the loss of Congress in midterm elections. The press opined that he was now lame duck and irrelevant. The president went on television and made a speech claiming that he was relevant. It was sort of pathetic that even the president of the United States, the most powerful person on the planet, wanted everyone to know he was relevant. This reflects the cultural need of many of us to have our importance constantly reinforced.

What if my résumé read something like this:

Bill Hull has been in ministry for thirty-four years. It has been marked by several apparent successes recognized by thousands of readers, parishioners, and conferees. But in his early fifties Bill found himself hungry for something more satisfying. He had been living a life based on a false identity carved out of public opinion. He was conducting his pastoral life based on principles and formulas. His foundation for daily ministry was a competence developed through hard work and faithfulness. Then God decided to break Bill through a series of trials, rejection of his ministry, lack of measurable success, personal pain, and repentance. In desperation Bill humbled himself before God not just in words but in practice by deciding to be irrelevant as Jesus was irrelevant and by daily deciding to follow Jesus and to lay aside the ways in which he used to measure success. Bill now

5. Nouwen, *In the Name of Jesus: Reflections on Christian Leadership* (New York: Crossroad, 1989), 17.

has plenty of free time to tell his story of how irrelevant and unnecessary he really is.

As I wrote in the chapter on submission, Jesus' irrelevancy is the most relevant quality to others for it is a humility that submits itself to loving and serving others, and that is the most powerful force known to any of us. So a choice to be irrelevant in the same way Jesus was irrelevant means to submit ourselves to his ways and means. In the *Unnecessary Pastor* Eugene Peterson gives three ways in which the pastor should be unnecessary:

1. Unnecessary to what culture says is important.
2. Unnecessary to what we ourselves feel is essential.
3. Unnecessary to what congregations insist we do for them.[6]

Unnecessary to What Culture Says Is Important

This is based on the Scripture, "Have this mind among yourselves, which is yours in Christ Jesus, who, though he was in the form of God, did not count equality with God a thing to be grasped" (Phil. 2:5–6 RSV). The issues we have already addressed in this chapter are "things to be grasped"—the rewards of both our culture and our religious communities. So we make a basic decision not to pursue them any longer, to change the source of our spiritual sustenance.

Culture tells us we are to be really nice people who open the Little League season with a prayer or say a benediction at the dedication of a new building site. Culture allows us to pepper people's lives with a little moral truth now and then to get them through the hard times. Most of all culture wants us to be chaplains, to marry, bury, and perform all the duties of our society. Whenever we accept this as our role, we are finished as spiritual leaders.

6. Eugene Peterson and Marva Dawn, *The Unnecessary Pastor* (Grand Rapids: Eerdmans, 2000), 2–5.

Jesus said, "I have come to bring fire on the earth" (Luke 12:49). We are called to be radical, but not in the mode and means of the world. Our radical nature is expressed in our stubborn insistence that we follow the humility and submission of Jesus in his agenda and ways of touching others. That way is to lead with a transformed character because character is influence.

Unnecessary to What We Ourselves Feel Is Essential

I have never been able to escape the feeling that I, as a pastor, am responsible for my church. It occurred to me one day that I was not *pastoring* the church as much as I was *running* the church. There are a number of reasons for believing this. The first is that when a pastor resigns, the church goes into a holding pattern while they search for a new pastor. Second, people expect leadership, and we attend seminars and read books on how to do it. If we do not lead, we are considered derelict, not gifted, or not blessed of God. Third, people measure the church's success by the pastor's performance and determine each week how things are going by the sermon.

It is for these reasons and more that we pastors feel somewhat indispensable and very important to the work. If I don't run this place, we might ask, who will? Our response should not be to become passive. Instead we need to consider how we lead and how we invest our time. If a church falls apart when we don't run it in the traditional sense, it proves that we were not building the ministry on the right foundation. We should ask ourselves what life would be like if we only did the things Scripture describes as essential for spiritual development.

Eugene Peterson was pastor of a Presbyterian church for many years. At one point he felt very strongly that he was engaging in nonpastoral activities that were expected of him but that he also felt were important in order to retain control. He made a decision to stop attending all committee meetings except for the elders' meeting. Some time later he dropped by a committee meeting and one of the members asked, "What are you doing here? Don't you trust us?" At that Peterson left and never returned because he realized he was unnecessary.

What would it be like if we could influence others through our character and teaching? What would it be like if who we are was so powerful that we didn't need organizational infrastructure to make things happen?

Unnecessary to What Congregations Insist We Do for Them

Congregations wait with bated breath for their new pastor, expecting him or her to ride in on a white charger to save the day and take the church to the next level. They are ready to make their impact, to become a large regional church, and to experience God's blessing. In other words, without knowing or articulating it, they have asked their new pastor to lead them into the world of religious competition. They want a pastor in the same way the Israelites wanted a king—they want a winner.

As a new pastor, you enter into the competitive world of what is hottest—the most exciting and most productive. If you don't believe this is paramount, watch what happens when people start streaming out the door to the hottest new thing. Do you feel the pressure? Of course you do. Do you feel like you are failing? Yes. Do you have an identity crisis and wonder where God's blessing has gone? You bet. Do people start to question your leadership? They do, and if you don't seem as panicked as they are, then you don't care, you're not open, you're not grow- ing, you've gone to seed.

Irrelevant and unnecessary—have you read a book on how to do that lately? There is not very much interest in humility and submission. We all give it the polite nod, but how many of us are really ready to choose to follow Jesus in this? But we cannot truly follow Jesus without committing to his commitment to humility and submission, to being irrelevant and unnecessary to what society (yes, even the religious society) values.

If you are still interested, let's move on to four steps forward. How can we reorder our lives as leaders?

1. GIVE UP THE GODS

Getting off the gods of our religious culture to which we are addicted is like going through detox. Their allure is so strong that it might require beginning with a complete separation from the conditions in which we live. That could be followed by a halfway house and practicing the new life with a strong support system.

My oldest son was caught up in the destructive nature of our culture. He was headed down the wrong road and was getting his needs for significance met in the wrong places. We sent him to a school for hard-to-parent teens for a year in the Dominican Republic. He didn't watch television or listen to the music of our culture; he lived without the noise and distraction. The total separation from his culture gave him a chance to get it all out of his system.

Please don't misunderstand me; we are not like confused teens living destructive lives. But we are leaders who love and desire to follow Jesus but are addicted to a religious culture that is not working for many of us. So what are the gods that must go?

Attendance

Many of the people who shaped my thinking are now long departed to a better life. But they left behind wonderful ideas in their books. One such pilgrim was a thoughtful Quaker named Elton Trueblood. Take in his comments about our worship of church attendance:

> If Christianity is primarily a matter of attendance at a performance, it is not different in kind from a host of other experiences. Though membership may include attendance at performances of a certain character, such attendance is not the primary meaning of the Christian effort at all. The fact that this is not generally understood is one of the chief evidences of the spiritual erosion which distresses us.[7]

7. Trueblood, *The Company of the Committed*, in Newby, *The Best of Elton Trueblood*, 112.

Trueblood thinks of the emphasis on church attendance as a pre-Christian idea. The feasts of Israel focused on getting as many people as possible to the temple on special occasions. The focus of the church is quite different. "The most important thing to God is the creation of centers of loving fellowships, which in turn infect the world. Whether the world can be redeemed in this way we don't know. But it is at least clear that there is no other way."[8] The focus of the church is to gather in order to inspire, encourage, comfort, train, and mobilize the members to penetrate their world. The kingdom is to grow naturally through families and other networks. The focus is the church in the world more than the church gathered for a meeting. The overemphasis on a "worship service" is not only a misunderstanding of worship itself but is a tyranny in which many feel trapped.

The single most important measure of success in our religious culture is attendance. We can deny it, but there is far too much evidence that this is the case. We honor and extol the largest churches. Their pastors become an elite priesthood to whom others look for guidance. And this belief system is crippling to the needed focus on what is required to fulfill the Great Commission.

I do not believe that pastors of large churches or the large churches themselves are the problem. In fact we should thank God for them and how they have helped us all. *What I am against is the belief that they are the standard by which we measure success.* The difference between the gathering of large groups in less than 3 percent of our churches and the natural expansion of the kingdom through millions of its members living out the life of Jesus is remarkable. Why should we be committed to what works 3 percent of the time and is dependent on personal charisma? It can't be reproduced, and it appeals to a motive that is less than healthy. We have reversed the flow that Scripture describes. The original churches met in homes and were kingdom outposts that stayed close to those who needed the gospel. The impulse

8. Ibid., 113.

to penetrate our world should be at least equal to the desire to gather for meetings.

One way to give up the god of attendance is to replace it with a different goal. Dallas Willard says it well, "We must flatly say that one of the greatest contemporary barriers to meaningful spiritual formation into Christlikeness is overconfidence in the spiritual efficacy of 'regular church services.' They are vital, they are not enough, it is that simple."[9]

When our goal changes from *recognition from others* to the *transformation of others*, it is easy to put attendance in its place. If I am committed to humility and submission, then being irrelevant and unnecessary to the gods of my culture is easy. My commitment and reward as a leader is enrolling members into the life and being a part of their transformation. That way every single leader can make it, succeed, and live out God's dream for him or her through who he or she is. Then attendance at meetings takes its place as one of the possible fruits of the work but not the ultimate proof of our talent and importance to God.

The Myth of Progress

The need to increase and make things happen is at epidemic levels. The original American Dream was freedom, liberty, and justice for all. After that was secured, it morphed into a materialistic dream. Now what people generally mean by the American Dream is that your children will live better than you did, that each subsequent generation will be richer, smarter, healthier, and happier.

The American church has been baptized by immersion in the American Dream, and we have stayed under a bit too long and become saturated in its philosophy. This means we expect the church to grow and improve its programs every year. The unforgivable sin is for a church to have a bad year. This is the

9. Dallas Willard, *Renovation of the Heart* (Colorado Springs: NavPress, 2002), 250.

myth of progress that was challenged by the late Christopher Lasch in *The True and Only Heaven.*

> How does it happen that serious people continue to believe in progress, in the face of massive evidence that might have been expected to refute the idea of progress once and for all? . . . Insatiable desire, formerly condemned as a source of frustration, unhappiness, and spiritual inability, came to be seen as a powerful stimulus to economic development. Instead of disparaging the tendency to want more than we need, liberals like Adam Smith argued that needs varied from one society to another, that civilized men needed more than savages to make them comfortable.[10]

Our culture is drenched with the competitive spirit. It started for me in Little League at age eight. I wanted to excel, and my popularity and self-worth were based on how I performed on the field. This followed me through my formative years and my athletic career and then went along for the ride into the pastoral life. Like most young pastors, my goals were scripturally based but driven by a personal need to succeed. This can cause our primary motivation to be competitive because we have been living in a false system. So instead of compassion being the earmark of our lives, we are caught up in trying to increase our influence and our ministry cachet.

Getting off this god is accomplished by adopting a new way of thinking. Henri Nouwen again helps us: "The way of Christian leadership is not the way of upward mobility in which our world has invested so much, but the way of downward mobility ending on the cross. Here we touch the most important quality of Christian leadership in the future. It is not a leadership of power and control; but a leadership of powerlessness and humility in which the suffering servant of God, Jesus Christ, is made manifest."[11]

10. Christopher Lasch, *The True and Only Heaven* (New York: Norton & Co., 1991), 13.
11. Nouwen, *In the Name of Jesus*, 62–63.

As John the Baptist immediately sensed when he saw Jesus, "He must increase, but I must decrease" (John 3:30 RSV). Isn't this freedom when we can lay aside the goals of increased salary, title, prestige, power, and influence? The hardest place to decrease is the influence and power we hold over people around us. Any leadership based on increasing the leader is wrong. But God does give increase and fruit, so by ripping the competitive spirit from our souls, we can see great increase in influence, prestige, and the like, but it is Christ's influence, not ours. Isn't that great? Think of it—whenever people want you to do ministry it is because Christ has increased in you and not because of you.

The Myth of Competence

Part of the esprit de corps of successful leaders is that they have the right stuff. There is a feeling when leaders gather: "We can relax now because we made the club. We are the elite who see things grow; we make things happen." It is true that such a gathering is one of talented beings. The myth for Christian leaders, however, is that a dependence on competence is in direct conflict with the kingdom value of brokenness.[12]

The leader's identity is shaped by his competence in making things happen. You may recall from the discussion in chapter 7 that a very competent leader may be standing on the very short Capacity Ladder (fig. 2, p. 134). He has accomplished much based on competence but now finds himself limited because his character has not developed along with his competence. So he must step across to a much taller Character Ladder (fig. 3, p. 136) and begin to climb. This is vital because we lead out of our character—our character is our influence. Competence can take you far, but it won't take you where God has planned for you to go. And what can be done with competence alone is puny and meager compared to a life that is lived out of the character of Christ in us.

12. My thanks to Judith Hougen and her fine work, *Transformed into Fire* (Grand Rapids: Kregel, 2003), 137.

The key to developing character is brokenness before God. This brokenness is a product of humility and submission. These are the very qualities that Jesus modeled as his core. In the competitive world brokenness is thought of as failure. When people speak of a person who changed his or her career and took less money or walked away from a more prestigious position, they say how they admire the individual, but you can tell by the look in their eye that they are not speaking with conviction. When leaders admit they are burned out or don't enjoy the pressure in the fast lane, the understood opinion is, "Too bad they didn't have the right stuff." In our culture that honors competence, brokenness is a delay or a disaster.

The myth of competence is the idea that we will outgrow our weaknesses, difficult sins, fears, and disappointments. We will reach a place of spiritual competence where *we have it together.* It's a myth because that time never comes; in fact our dependence on God grows as we become more like Jesus. Brokenness is living life in light of that reality.

Don't godly people get over their brokenness? Apparently the apostle Paul didn't; he spoke about his thorn in the flesh:

> Concerning this thing I pleaded with the Lord three times that it might depart from me. And He said to me, "My grace is sufficient for you, for My strength is made perfect in weakness." Therefore most gladly I will rather boast in my infirmities, that the power of Christ may rest upon me. Therefore I take pleasure in infirmities, in reproaches, in needs, in persecutions, in distresses, for Christ's sake. For when I am weak, then I am strong.
>
> 2 Corinthians 12:8–10 NKJV

The same Greek word is translated "weakness" in verse 9 and "infirmities" twice in verse 10. I believe the best translation is *weakness.* Paul uses the thorn in the flesh as a focus point and then extrapolates a larger meaning from it. He gladly boasts about his weakness—it is out in the open. He isn't shamed by his lack of competence or abilities. He led with his lack of abilities: "I came to you in weakness and fear, and with much trembling" (1 Cor. 2:3).[13]

Even Jesus honored his own wounds; he carried with him in his resurrected body the scars of crucifixion. The disciples could see and touch his wounds. The wounds of life are real—our inabilities are there for people to see. Leading with our weakness, with our wounds, is a powerful way to touch those around us. We don't lead as a wounded victim but as one who has found an answer in Christ who heals us and enables us to live with and through our needs. It is in this humility that our lives find their real power because God's power becomes mature or perfect in a person's weakness.

Our culture accepts the god of competence, which says that pain and suffering is failure, that someone who struggles with fear and rejection is not walking with God. If they have these problems, then something has gone wrong—they made a mistake, they didn't listen, they didn't read the right books. Those who accept the god of competence never really stop to remember that Jesus struggled; he was rejected; he failed in some of his work; he was considered a zealous idiot by many.

Competence is a barrier; it makes people who see themselves as less competent feel that you don't understand them and, therefore, you cannot help them. My image of competence came through much stronger than my need of God's help, and it became my greatest barrier to connecting with others. My wife, Jane, has told me that the reason I "tick some people off" is that I make work look easy. When God broke me, he gave me words to express that brokenness in a way that got through to those around me. Then the real power of ministry came into my life, my preaching, and my personal interaction. They could see me as one of them—a fellow believer struggling daily to live out the life that Christ lived. What a glorious day when I realized that Paul's wonderful words of honoring weakness were talking about me.

13. Paul says he did not use persuasive words or great wisdom but only the simple power of God (1 Cor. 2:1–5).

There may be many other ways to describe the gods we serve, but it is a good starting point to give up the gods of attendance, the need for progress, and the myth of competence. Then we can move on to a new way of being, thinking, and doing. The unnecessary and irrelevant leader is the leader who follows Jesus in the way Jesus lived and taught. Therefore, he or she is worthy of the name *disciple*. The next step is to fill the vacuum left by giving up our gods.

2. DEVELOP YOUR INNER LIFE

Henri Nouwen said, "The central question at the heart of Christian leadership is, are the leaders of the future truly men and women of God, people with an ardent desire to dwell in God's presence, to listen to God's voice, to look at God's beauty, to touch God's incarnate Word, and to taste fully God's infinite goodness?"[14] Did you notice the qualities Nouwen mentions?

- dwell in God's presence
- listen to God's voice
- focus on God's beauty
- taste God's goodness

These describe a level of experience with God that could be new to many of us, and it begins with personal time with God. I am not talking now about the typical quiet time, because to be honest, mine were too often just me doing religious stuff with very little experience. I find when I am rushed I fall back into the same superficiality of doing things *about* God rather than meeting *with* God.

Are you ready to face down your weakness, to uncover the stuff hidden in the darkness? It started for me with a word from God, "Bill, I'm going to break you. Don't run." When I first heard God

14. Nouwen, *In the Name of Jesus*, 29–30.

say this, I did not fully realize what he meant. I had so romanticized the concept of brokenness that I saw it as an event with a beginning and an end rather than a process—a state of being.

Being a self-disciplined, well-educated leader with an acceptable quiet time wasn't sufficient to develop the qualities extolled by Henri Nouwen. I had spent thirty years developing my skills and producing many good things, which God had blessed. But as I wrote in chapter 4, I had to submit myself in humility to train to be godly. That training needed to be in developing my inner life. I made a decision to follow Jesus instead of leading him.

Being and Doing

A common construct used to explain the difference between the inner life and the outer life, is *being and doing*. Now it may be true that our *doing* comes from our *being*, but we cannot separate the two. In fact our doing impacts our being because if we pray for God to bless someone we detest, it will change our attitude about the person. So in that case doing something transformed our being. But deeds are not paramount to transformation; it is the inner play between the two that makes life work.

I like the words of Abraham Joshua Heschel on this subject:

> The world needs more than the secret holiness of individual inwardness. It needs more than sacred sentiments and good intentions. God asks for the heart because he needs the lives. It is by lives that the world will be redeemed, by lives that beat in concordance with God, by deeds that outbeat the finite charity of the human heart. *Man's power of action is less vague than his power of intention.* And an action has intrinsic meaning; its value to the world is independent of what it means to the person performing it. The giving of food to a helpless child is meaningful regardless of whether or not the moral intention is present. God asks for the heart, and we must spell our answer in terms of deeds.[15]

15. Abraham Joshua Heschel, *God in Search of Man*, in *A Guide to Prayer for Ministers and Other Servants*, comp. Rueben P. Job and Norman Shawchuck (Nashville: Upper Room, 1983), 133.

It would be safe to say that the claim that purity of heart is the exclusive test of piety is a destructive heresy. It would be just as damaging to believe that actions that are derived from simple human goodness are sufficient to transform the world. It will take a heart response to God to sustain lives of sacrifice. So the practical solution for the journey ahead is to do something that transforms our being.

Live from a Satisfied Soul

There is a template for us to follow in reordering our lives and that is Psalm 23. "The LORD is my shepherd; I shall not want" (Ps. 23:1 NKJV). The primary strength of a spiritual leader is a satisfied soul, with which one can lead a very powerful life. On the other hand, to live out of unmet need usually results in dissatisfaction on the part of the leader and the ones he or she leads.

Pastoral or organizational leaders are trained to make an impact. I have spent so much of my life wanting to do better, to accomplish more. My earliest days out of college I was trained to think that God's will is always doing what will reach the most people. Therefore, my decisions were driven by numbers—going to the place where the most people would be touched by my ministry. After years of having quantity be the guiding force of my life, when the mission was shrinking rather than growing, where could I go to get my needs met? Good performance gives good rewards, but when the rewards stop, you start running on empty or on fading memories of results in a previous work. So my personal experience was one of dissatisfaction. Either I was seeing results but was driven to see more, or it wasn't going well and I was in crisis. There was very little rest in my soul.

What I have described is very common for leaders. We want, we desire, we claw, and we climb. We have never come to terms with the real source of satisfaction. The interesting thing is that people around us honor this drivenness by calling it "holy dissatisfaction."

Rethinking Who I Am as a Leader

When the Lord is my Shepherd, my Leader, I will be contented. This does not mean passiveness; it means God is in control of the results. I give the effort; he uses it as he pleases. In fact, my personal joy is not based on outcomes; it is based on his love and goodness. I abdicate the responsibility to make things happen. My focus is not primarily to figure out what is happening in my culture or to strategize; it is to follow my Leader's ways of being and doing. My Shepherd is Jesus; he knows my voice, and I know his (John 10:14). The first and most important thing I can do is commit myself to learn how to hear his voice, to enjoy his presence, to experience an intimacy with him that itself is transformational. This is the part most of us have skipped; we went directly to giving our all for the cause. Amazingly, God loves us and has rewarded us and blessed us in spite of the fact that we have often ignored him.

So who am I as a leader? I am at the core a follower and one who starts with God. I start with a commitment to dwell, listen, focus, and taste. To dwell in his presence, to listen to his voice, to focus on his beauty, and to taste his goodness. Then there is nothing left to want. All my wanting becomes the flesh rearing its very attractive head. And it will on a regular basis. The last thing most of us need to worry about is being impractically passive by spending too much time contemplating God. That impulse, that push to do, is there all the time and it works so much better when we do from a place of being filled, contented; then it is sustained and under the Shepherd's control. This then becomes my new engine; it is what is under the hood.

God Makes My Doing Come from My Being

These familiar words reach deep within me when I read them: "He makes me to lie down in green pastures; He leads me beside the still waters. He restores my soul" (Ps. 23:2–3 NKJV). I don't have any personal experience in herding sheep; I only know what I have read. But it makes perfect sense that sheep thrive on certain things. They love pastures of tender green grass and the quiet waters of a small stream. Sheep are easily frightened, and it is in that environment that restoration takes place from the traumas of life. The shepherd knows they need times of rest and nourishment to counterbalance the attacks from other animals and periods of deprivation from food and drink.

God does the same for us. He knows that we need places of nourishment and rest. The pastures God provides never run out of grass and the streams never run dry.

SILENCE AND SOLITUDE

Leaders don't seem to appreciate what we need the most, but God knows. When we change our basic mode of operation from the belief that our hard work and strategies are what make things happen, it changes our core behavior. This reorganization requires that we begin with silence and solitude—the primary starting point for a leader who wants to be transformed by God and to lead others into the same experience. Our core behavior then is to follow our Leader as he guides us to prayer and reflection, to quietness, and to listening skills that will satisfy and restore our souls. God says, "Lie down here where it is quiet, where I can talk to you, where you can hear what I have to say." This is counterintuitive for the high achiever, so I want to affirm to all high achievers the truth that solitude is action! Henri Nouwen wrote that solitude is the furnace of transformation.[16]

Solitude is the basic spiritual discipline. Without it you will be hindered in everything else you try. Reading Scripture in spiritual depth is not very effective unless done alone. This practice breaks the back of self-sufficiency—the need to be in control and in the fray. If we give Jesus his way and follow his example, he will say, "Stop here first. Sit a while and let's get on the same page."

16. Henri J. M. Nouwen, *The Way of the Heart: Desert Spirituality and Contemporary Ministry* (New York: Seabury, 1981).

CONTEMPLATION AS NONACTIVITY

There is something deeply embedded in us that makes silence and solitude, the lying beside still waters motif, seem like loafing. Or at most we consider it a necessary prelude to the real stuff, like an invocation before the championship game. The struggle then is for my core belief to develop parallel to my core behavior. So my core belief must see a connection between what happens when I am with God alone and what happens when I am working for God.

There are two ways to think about this connection. The first would be the pattern of thinking that the longer we pray, the more fruit in the ministry. If we fast and pray one day a week, then our churches will grow 20 percent next year instead of 10 percent. We then assume that a successful person must have a devoted prayer life. We make the connection that amounts of prayer make more stuff happen. While this is an attractive idea, this makes spending time with God another church growth technique.

Now I must admit that there is so much mystery in and around prayer that I won't make categorical statements about this dimension. Sometimes there may very well be a correlation between amounts of prayer and results. I recall the statement of E. M. Bounds that it is not how much we pray but how much of us is in the prayer. It may be that believing, heartfelt prayer is a key. Others might advocate *lectio divina*—a reading of Scripture with the heart so God can speak to you. Sometimes the reason we spend time with God is really about our goals more than it is about a relationship.

The second way to think about silence and solitude is that it is the best environment for contemplative and deep prayer. The connection is not about the growth of ministry but about the transformation of the person. When our intimacy with God is deepened, we hear his voice, we learn to enjoy his presence, we taste his goodness and mercy, and he changes our character. Through humility and submission we now allow him to lead us. We understand more about his ways and his means of touching others. So our transformed character begins to touch others in a new way that is attractive. And then more and more people are attracted to how Christ is working in us. We lead with our own brokenness, and the impact is greater.

So silence and solitude along with other disciplines are the means God uses to transform us. A critical change in ethos for the leader is the changing of connections. Think of it as rewiring our connections. Disconnect the wire between a devotional life and numerical results in finance or followers and reroute it to connect the devotional life to personal character formed by Christ. Then influence comes from the Christlike character and radiates out to those in the sphere of influence. That influence will be stronger and there will be better results because it is the character of Christ in us.

RESTORATION OF THE SOUL

The experience of silence and solitude will then restore our souls (Ps. 23:3). The Hebrew word for *restore* means "to bring it back." One must ask where it has been. It has been wandering and found other places for rest and comfort. Isn't this what happens to us when we lose our closeness to God by not spending time with him? We get away from the green pastures and still waters where the soul's sustenance resides. The other pastures and streams are not satisfying. The other options provide thrills for the soul, but they do not give spiritual nourishment. They are filled with empty promises that damage and disappoint our souls. They numb our souls and lead them away from humility and submission and encourage pride and a take-control attitude. Again Henri Nouwen speaks eloquently to this, "The long painful history of the Church is people ever and again tempted to choose power over love, control over the cross, being a leader over being led."[17] This is what happens when we forget God's character and his ways.

17. Nouwen, *In the Name of Jesus*, 60.

If we are praised for our achievements in ministry, we can be in danger of our souls feeding in the pasture of adulation and ego gratification. We drink the waters of self-importance and start grasping for that which Christ did not grasp. If we become accustomed to adulation, then not to be mentioned or acknowledged causes a wound and can lead to anger and a sarcastic spirit toward the evangelical fame machine. Affirmation can be a wonderful thing, but if we come to expect praise, it may require a significant time in God's pasture drinking the right water in order to restore the damage done.

As part of my quest to understand more about the history of spiritual formation, I read *The Spiritual Exercises of St. Ignatius*. I didn't think much of the exercises that called for contemplation of bodies burning in hell, the wearing of hair shirts or chains, or flogging myself with a whip. But there was a passage that struck me as helpful, even though it goes further than Scripture requires. "We should not prefer health to sickness, riches to poverty, honor to dishonor, a long life to a short life. . . . Man is created to praise, reverence and serve God our Lord, and by this means to save his soul."[18] I must say that I do prefer health to sickness, riches to poverty, and a long life to a short one, but the force of the passage is total surrender, and that I do desire. I also find myself a kindred spirit when it comes to the honor and dishonor challenge. It is only in the enjoyment of God's presence that we find the kind of strength to be totally surrendered.

The primary work of a pastor or spiritual leader is to live a life of the restored soul, which comes from time in the green pastures and still waters of his presence. A restored soul is a satisfied soul, and people around us will know it. They will desire the same freedom from spiritual fast food, from slavery to self, from the need to perform in order to fill the emptiness inside. This is the lodestar for the passionate spirituality so desperately needed by all of us. I can't prove it to you with hard data or numerical analysis, but when you experience it, you are transformed.

18. Louis Puhl, *The Spiritual Exercises of St. Ignatius* (New York: Random House, 2000), 12.

My Leader or Shepherd, Jesus, has satisfied me. I am not in want of any of the rewards that he finds not worthy to be grasped. My brokenness—which is a state of being, a daily process—provides for me a restored soul. This is why Jesus said we must take up our cross daily and follow him (Luke 9:23). It is out of this relationship then that I follow his leadership.

God Leads Me in the Paths of Righteousness

There is liberty and confidence in knowing that God "leads me in the paths of righteousness for His name's sake" (Ps. 23:3 NKJV). This eliminates doubt in troubled times and is a sustaining influence when we might otherwise wonder if we've taken the right path. Doubts and fears cannot survive in a person's soul when he or she is dwelling in God's presence, hearing his voice, and tasting his goodness.

So how is this life on the path of righteousness lived out? Chapters 7 and 8 dealt with the interpersonal and community dynamics of how to live out the life of discipleship. Here we will focus on how following Jesus in this new way looks in leaders. We will assume the leaders have chosen the life of discipleship and have reordered their lives by admitting that something is not right and choosing a different kind of being. So the leaders have given up their gods and now have given themselves to the development of their inner lives. The spiritual disciplines are now a regular part of their lives. There is one primary characteristic that makes this new ethos work: *I wait for God to create the ministry in front of me before I act.*

The paths of righteousness are of course moral paths, but they are also life directional, and when we follow we can be confident that it will be for "His name's sake" (Ps. 23:3 NKJV). St. Ignatius advocated the removal of all personal desire, but as human beings we probably can't go that far. We can, however, focus on the higher reality where ministry is for God and not us.

In the early years of my ministry, my decision-making process could be described in this way:

- I am filled with the Spirit.
- Therefore, whatever my desires are, they will be blessed of God (2 Sam. 7:3).
- I have an idea, create a strategy, seek counsel, raise the money, recruit the personnel, set a timetable, and launch.
- Tweak, learn, tweak, learn more, make sure it grows, and if it doesn't grow, figure out why and fix it.

The way it is now for me:

- Spend extended times with God, listen to his voice, dwell in his presence to build my passion and sensitivity to his Spirit. Ask him to reveal his plan and path.
- When I see God working out in front of me, I pray about that path whether it be invitations to teach, opportunities to serve, or people sent into my life to help me see new paths.
- I ask God for a desire that is consistent with the proper path (Phil. 2:13). He works in me "to will" and then "to work" for his good pleasure. Is God putting the will in me to do some kind of work?
- I ask God directly about any desires and ideas I have. I hear his voice through the Scriptures, the counsel of others, and circumstances.
- I ask for God's confirmation that the path is the right one through the supply of resources, personnel, and opportunity.
- Only then do I take any action.

As an example of this decision-making process, over two years ago I was invited to a meeting of leaders concerned about the lack of transformation in the American church. I was hesitant at first because I already had a busy life as a pastor, but I decided to attend because a friend invited me and a number of disciple-making writers and leaders were planning to be there. It was a good meeting and the ideas were interesting, but frankly no one there had any suggestions as to what to do. I committed to pray about it and see if God would stir my heart. Over a period of months God began to create a desire in me to be with those men again. Then one day the leader of the group called me and said he wanted to come visit me. He didn't really know why; he just sensed he should. I didn't tell him, but I was beginning to sense that God was increasing my passion for this concern. He and I struck up a friendship and began to talk on the phone about our growing passion.

I started preaching on the subject of spiritual transformation, and the congregation took to it so strongly that I was very surprised. I began to see confirmations in the leadership of the church, the members, and the staff. It seemed as though God had prepared the entire church for the message. God began to work in front of me, and suddenly there was a flurry of speaking engagements. Whenever I spoke on Choose the Life, they too responded unlike anything I had ever seen.

Within a year my desire had grown so intense it became a daily issue in my pastoral work. I realized that I couldn't continue to live a divided life. I needed to choose between two things I loved: the pastoral life or being a voice to the church at large. God spoke to me very clearly, telling me to choose based on the will he had put into me, which would drive the work I was to do. I left behind the security and blessings of the pastoral life in order to become a discipleship evangelist, evangelizing the church to choose the life of discipleship and follow Jesus into transformation. God confirmed this through providing our financial needs and the blessing and laying on of hands of the group of leaders with whom I worked.

I was careful to follow Jesus and not lead him on this because I am now a committed follower rather than a leader. My only influence is as Jesus' character comes through me to reach others. We must reach new heights of trust to follow Jesus because if we fear, we will find it impossible to follow him to the places he wants to lead us.

Trouble Is the Crucible of Transformation

"Yea, though I walk through the valley of the shadow of death" (Ps. 23:4 NKJV) doesn't refer to the death of the psalmist but to living under its shadow. It could be the death of someone close to us, a near-death experience, or our own impending death. Regardless, it is not a mountaintop experience; it is a valley. This psalm has been precious to many because it brings comfort in the most difficult times of life. It is the confidence that is described so beautifully, "I will fear no evil; for You are with me; Your rod and Your staff, they comfort me" (Ps. 23:4 NKJV).

God is present in a stronger way when we are in trouble. The assurance of his presence that is experienced deep within our spirit gives us a sense of invulnerability in a time when we are most vulnerable. We are invulnerable because we are not influenced by anyone other than God, and that takes away the fear of evil and at the same time provides comfort. Add to that the assurance that God works all things together for good to those who love God and are called according to his purpose and the fact that pressure produces perseverance, which builds our character, then we know why we don't fear evil (Rom. 8:28; James 1:2–4). Then we can say with confidence that there is no change that God wants to make in our lives that we should fear.

CHARACTER DEVELOPMENT THROUGH TROUBLE

Earlier I said that character is developed in community. This means that life is an inner play between being and doing. My inner life informs my actions, and my actions help form my inner life. I have advocated that as leaders we reorder our lives by giving up our gods and giving ourselves to the development of our inner lives. A major part of that reordering is the development of a strong practice of the spiritual disciplines. I have also stated that spiritual disciplines are to character transformation what calisthenics are to sport. They are tools that God provides in order to create the opportunity for inner transformation. But transformation of our character is developed as we begin to live out our new values among others. Just as our humility is tested in submission, our love is tested when others treat us unkindly. Our selflessness is tested when we are slighted, and our patience is tested when circumstances don't improve.

So your ministry isn't going well. Your projected growth has not come. Finances are beginning to get thin, and so is the patience of those you lead. You are beginning to doubt your plan, your skills, your calling, your God. The gods you just recently forsook are pulling at you. The attendance god is looming large; the need for progress growing; your ego is running about looking for a place to be fed. Your mind begins to wonder what colleagues are saying—"Oh, Joe is having trouble; I didn't think he was up to it."

Trouble is the intersection where the necessary, relevant leader and the unnecessary, irrelevant leader collide. The temptation is to revert to the default position and abandon the new, idyllic notion of leading from the inner life. Every normal indicator will tell you, "You are failing." This is the leader's valley of the shadow, the shadow of the ruin of a ministry or a career. The fear becomes palpable; you want to run from it because it looks like failure.

There is hope and help that will enable us to create a new ethos. This is when we refocus by not running from the problems but diving headfirst into them. We run to God and dwell in his presence; we listen to his voice; we focus on his beauty; we taste his goodness. By doing this, we can turn back the gods of attendance and the need for progress and making things happen, for "I will fear no evil" (Ps. 23:4 NKJV). We can believe he loves us and will make something grand out of this experience, and we can trust that we are going to become more like him through it, and that will enhance our influence. "For you are with me" (Ps. 23:4 NKJV). We are not alone; we are dwelling in his presence. He is applauding because we have chosen his way. Then comes his comfort; he restores our souls that have been traumatized by the experience. His rod and staff are metaphors from the life of the shepherd; his rod provides us with protection, and his staff is the guidance of the Holy Spirit.

Success Can Bring Trouble

You will also find your commitment to transformation challenged during periods of success, because nothing fails like success. It can distract us from the goal of following Jesus. The religious culture's system of rewards and punishments can entrap you when you are being rewarded. The gods are lavishing you with fame. People are coming to you for advice. You are invited to travel and share your wisdom. It seems as though the Holy Spirit has kissed your lips and you are flying high for God. It is hard to hear God's voice in such times.

The problem in this case is not the rewards and opportunities, it is trying to keep a grip on who is exalting you. If you have already chosen the life of following Jesus, meaning you have committed to humility and submission, then the rewards might be his exaltation. But such rewards can distract you from your devotion to Christ. They can build pride and hubris so you can't hear his voice. Can you think of a greater trouble than a leader of great influence who is not listening to God? My experience is that the more successful we are in the world system, the more our confidence in ourselves grows. We get used to being treated like a celebrity, and we start to act like a prima donna. The pride we feel when we are with the less successful is a devilish cancer that eats away at our Christlikeness.

I have had many encounters with leaders on the rise and there is one common denominator: They don't listen well. They are focused on talking about their success. Their attitude towards those who have not succeeded is polite and dismissive. It seems as though the large and powerful in Christianity only respect the strength of size. This is very human, but it is a block to hearing what God has to say to us through others and even in times of prayer. So consider this a warning to the successful that success can become its own trouble because it is the natural enemy of humility and submission.

The Resource to Resist Reverting

Let's say that you are experiencing liberation from the prevailing trends of contemporary success. So you can faithfully lead from a place of personal confidence that following Jesus' example is better in the long run than following other gods. God's presence in your life overpowers the Enemy's presence.

"You prepare a table before me in the presence of my enemies; You anoint my head with oil; my cup runs over" (Ps. 23:5 NKJV). These words describe for the leader a life of confidence in following Jesus in spite of the surrounding culture and even religious culture. God prepares a feast in the middle of the enemy camp. I picture the leader telling people that attendance at our meetings is down, giving has taken a dip, but I am confident and secure to continue following a different way. I am even anointed, and my personal joy is like a cup running over. It reminds me of Jesus' declaration at the Feast of Tabernacles when the priest poured water over the altar, "If anyone thirsts, let him come to Me and drink. He who believes in Me, as the Scripture has said, out of his heart will flow rivers of living water" (John 7:37–38 NKJV).

We have the inner resources to hang tough when the temptation is to move away from the development of the inner life because it doesn't seem to be working. Jesus' methods and priorities were not understood by his followers and were, in fact, rejected by them in many cases. His family and the religious leaders didn't grasp his values of how personal character and depth are the key in the long run to delivering the life of the kingdom to the needy.

Henri Nouwen said, "Joy and sorrow are the parents of our spiritual growth."[19] Those who persevere have a deeply embed-

19. Henri J. M. Nouwen, *Bread for the Journey* (New York: HarperCollins, 1997), entry for January 2.

ded mind-set: "Surely goodness and mercy shall follow me all the days of my life; and I will dwell in the house of the LORD forever" (Ps. 23:6 NKJV). This is a lesson learned in the crucible of pain. When we give up living based upon our judgments about success and failure, we are approaching liberation.

Can we imagine a life that is an offering to God regardless of outcome, leaving the results to God? Those around us will not consider pain and suffering a success. But those who have walked through the valley of the shadow, who have stuck with it and have been comforted, will take on an attitude of hope and optimism. Their lives proclaim: God is smiling; he is with me. His goodness and mercy have filled my cup, and if you get close to me, my joy will spill onto you.

3. GIVE YOURSELF TO THE PRINCIPLE OF DISCIPLESHIP

Christ existed for others. When we take on his form we begin to see the connection between the inner life and the outer life. It is inescapable. If Jesus exists for others, then his followers exist for others, and the church community exists for others. It is in this selfless act that we can meet our own needs. When we have changed our mode of leadership, when we begin to minister out of satisfaction rather than want, the spirit's impulse is to affect others. In fact, I would think anyone filled with God would burst if they couldn't.

The Command and Curriculum

The kingdom of God is meant to grow through the principle of discipleship. The principle is the impact of one life on others—the character, skill, and perspective of one godly person passed on to another willing person. The command and curriculum is "teaching them to obey everything I commanded you" (Matt. 28:20). Jesus commanded 212 things, which provides us with a very rich curriculum. The aim of the teaching is obedience, which should encourage those of us who believe that faith is action sustained by belief. As leaders we cannot be satisfied with just talking about what Jesus commanded, but we must be committed to living it out in community with others. "For this is the love of God, that we keep his commandments. And his commandments are not burdensome" (1 John 5:3 RSV).

Because character is developed in community, you can't make disciples without accountability. That accountability should be relationships of trust in an environment of grace. Accountability without trusting relationships will feel militaristic and will not last long. Unless there are relationships of trust, our unresolved sin, guilt, and shame will dive deeper into the hidden places of our souls where they will remain unhealed and will resurface later in damaging ways.

Discipleship that is lived out in community provides a balance of time alone with God and time with others. They work together and, in fact, are of equal importance. We are to live out Jesus' commands in a community of grace in which there is a common commitment to follow Jesus and to help others to do the same. Following is a representative list of his commands:

Love one another as I have loved you (John 13:34–35).
Bless those who persecute you (Matt. 5:11–12).
Esteem one another (1 Thess. 5:13).
Comfort one another (1 Thess. 5:14).
Forgive one another (Matt. 6:12, 15).
Confess your sins to one another (James 5:16).
Agree in prayer with each other (Matt. 18:19–20).
Love your neighbor (Matt. 22:39).

The curriculum is not only everything Jesus commanded but also everything he did and the way he lived. Please recall the conditions of Christian discipleship found in chapter 2:

1. A disciple submits to a teacher who teaches him or her how to follow Jesus.
2. A disciple learns Jesus' words.
3. A disciple learns Jesus' way of ministry.
4. A disciple imitates Jesus' life and character.
5. A disciple finds and teaches other disciples.

The Method

The command is to be and make disciples, which means "teaching them to obey everything I commanded you" (Matt. 28:20). The method is tried and true: Teach faithful people who in turn will be able to teach others (2 Tim. 2:2). This means that as a leader I will choose to invest my best effort in developing faithful leaders who will be able to reproduce. This also means that a good deal of my time could be spent meeting with a few in order to have a larger impact later.

It has been my belief for many years that it is the neglect of this simple process that is behind our weakness as a church. This neglect has been largely due to pastors and other leaders not having the patience and commitment to the process. It is just too tempting to build a large congregation faster through preaching. For those who can draw large crowds, there are very tangible rewards in being known as a great communicator.

Our behavior reveals what we really care about, and sadly, in too many cases that is success in numbers and recognition of our skills. This must be cast off and abandoned by those leaders who want to follow Jesus. We should keep preaching and strategizing the best we can, but we must put our best effort into the training of faithful leaders. Staff meetings and occasional leadership retreats don't cut it. It must be a sustained effort one-on-one or in groups of three or four in order to develop the best results. Listen to Paul's advice to Timothy and to the Philippian believers:

> Now you have observed my teaching, my conduct, my aim in life, my faith, my patience, my love, my steadfastness, my persecu-

tions, my sufferings, what befell me at Antioch, at Iconium, and at Lystra, what persecutions I endured; yet from them all the Lord rescued me. . . . But as for you, continue in what you have learned and firmly believed, *knowing from whom you have learned it.*

2 Timothy 3:10, 14 RSV, emphasis added

What you have learned and received and heard and seen in me, do; and the God of peace will be with you.

Philippians 4:9 RSV

These passages scream relationship, doing the work together, spending time together, knowing each other intimately.

I often think of the words of Elton Trueblood when it comes to this kind of investment:

There is no person in history who has impacted all of mankind more than Jesus of Nazareth. Jesus was deeply concerned for the continuation of his redemptive, reconciling work after the close of his earthly existence, and his chosen method was the formation of a small band of committed friends. He did not form an army, establish a headquarters, or even write a book. What he did was to collect a few very common men and women, inspire them with the sense of his spirit and vision, and build their lives into an intensive fellowship of affection, worship and work.

One of the truly shocking passages of the gospel is that in which Jesus indicates that there is absolutely no substitute for the tiny, loving, caring, reconciling society. If this fails, he suggests, all is failure; there is no other way. He told the little bedraggled fellowship that they were actually the salt of the earth and that if this salt should fail there would be no adequate preservative at all. He was staking all on one throw.

What we need is not intellectual theorizing or even preaching, but a demonstration. One of the most powerful ways of turning people's loyalty to Christ is by loving others with the great love of God. We cannot revive faith by argument, but we might catch the imagination of puzzled men and women by an exhibition of a fellowship so intensely alive that every thoughtful person would be forced to respect it. If there should emerge in our day such a fellowship, wholly without artificiality and free from the dead hand of the past, it would be an exciting event of momentous importance. A society of genuine loving friends, set free from the self seeking struggle for personal prestige and from all unreality, would be something unutterably priceless and powerful. A wise person would travel any distance to join it.[20]

What Jesus taught and modeled, which was imitated by Paul with Timothy and others, is the most powerful force for change. It is the influence of one person's character on another. As Henri Nouwen said, "The greatest gift I have to offer is my own joy of living, my own inner peace, my own silence and solitude, my own sense of well-being."[21] As Trueblood put it, "A wise person would travel any distance to join it."[22] Peter did, John did, Matthew did, Timothy did, Titus did, Luke did, and many of you reading this book did. There is nothing like it anywhere—the power of a transformed life.

This is the reason the principle of discipleship is God's way to reach the world. In fact it is the only way to reach the world. God has put each of us into the middle of the harvest field as "insiders"[23] so our lives can speak to those around us. That is the way the kingdom is to grow, through the natural means of one life on another. This gets at the heart of this book's thesis: *A transformed life is needed, a life of depth of true disciples who have chosen to follow the life that Jesus lived. The reason the mission languishes is the acceptance of a nondiscipleship Christianity that creates shallow believers with hollow lives who don't affect those around them. This has led to the marginalization of the gospel and has retarded its spread because of its lack of authenticity and power.*

20. Excerpts from Trueblood, in Newby, *The Best of Elton Trueblood*.
21. Henri J. M. Nouwen, *The Life of the Beloved* (New York: Crossroad, 1992), 90.
22. Trueblood, in Newby, *The Best of Elton Trueblood*.
23. I recommend Jim Petersen and Mike Shamy, *The Insider: Bringing the Kingdom of God into Your Everyday World* (Colorado Springs: NavPress, 2003).

Are you the kind of leader whose life has a positive effect on those around you? We must each start with ourselves. Take off the leadership garb for a moment and ask yourself, Who am I impacting for Christ from my life, not from my position? If it were not my job to reach people for Christ, would I try? Is there any evidence outside of my professional efforts to prove it? Am I leading others by the example of my life (1 Peter 5:1–6)? As Paul so boldly put it, "Follow my example, as I follow the example of Christ" (1 Cor. 11:1). Be a faithful leader who teaches others. Start small and think big, and in time it will work better than anything you have ever tried. Your joyful love for others can penetrate any barrier the world, the flesh, or the Enemy can erect.

4. Give Yourself to Others

What do we give to others? Give them who Christ is in you and teach them to follow him as you have learned to follow him. I have four recommendations:

1. Enroll yourself in study and practice of the spiritual disciplines.
2. Enroll a few select people in the process with you.
3. Teach it to everyone in your community.
4. Create a society of the willing.

Study and Practice the Spiritual Disciplines

There are various streams of theological education. Mine has been primarily evangelical, which means my exposure to much of the spiritual formation literature was meager. I suggest the following reading regime to introduce yourself to much valuable spiritual formation literature.

For the Concepts and Ideas

The Cost of Discipleship, by Dietrich Bonhoeffer
The Company of the Committed, by Elton Trueblood

The Spirit of the Disciplines, by Dallas Willard

The Divine Conspiracy, by Dallas Willard

Celebration of Discipline, by Richard Foster

The Unnecessary Pastor, by Eugene Peterson and Marva Dawn

The Mentored Life, by James Houston

Working the Angles, by Eugene Peterson

FOR THE DEVOTIONAL LIFE

Devotional Classics, edited by Richard Foster (introductory readings from the classic spiritual writers)

A Guide to Prayer for Ministers and Other Servants, compiled by Rueben P. Job and Norman Shawchuck (based on the liturgical year with many good readings from classic writers)

THE CLASSICS

Imitation of Christ, by Thomas à Kempis

The Rule of St. Benedict

The Confessions of St. Augustine

The Private Devotions of Lancelot Andrewes

The Devotions of John Donne

The Pensées of Blaise Pascal

Introduction to the Devout Life, by Francis de Sales

Purity in Heart, by Søren Kierkegaard

The Spiritual Exercises of St. Ignatius

The benefit of reading these books is to enter another world filled with mystery and heart devotion. It is interesting that these writers were scholars with great minds and lives of discipline, yet their writing is from and speaks to the heart in a way that is foreign to us. One must make allowance for excessive theological beliefs and practices suitable only to such a time as they wrote, but if you discard the hair shirts and self-flagellation, there is much from which to benefit. Reading and meditating on the classics can cultivate a heart for God.

You can also learn various approaches to prayer that can bring your time with God alive. The idea that Bible reading and prayer can be one thing rather than two has been very helpful to me. The process called *lectio divina*, or sacred reading, is worth your investigation. Bruce Demarest summarizes it, "*Lectio divina* proceeds in four stages. In the language of the centuries they are *lectio* [reading], *meditatio* [discursive meditation], *oratio* [affective prayer], and *contemplatio* [contemplation]." Demarest goes on to describe each stage,

> *Lectio.* First select a Scripture passage, take a short section and then with a listening heart read the text aloud slowly and deliberately. When you find a word or phrase or sentence that speaks to your heart, pause in your reading.
>
> *Meditatio.* Second, meditate or mull over the word or words. Allow God to settle it into your soul. Allow the words to probe your attitude, emotions, and aspirations.
>
> *Oratio.* Third, return the Scripture you have just read to the Father by praising him for its work in you. Talk to the Father about your reading.
>
> *Contemplatio.* The final stage is resting in the Lord's presence. This is the act of simply being with God.[24]

I encourage you to explore new vistas of the devotional life that we as evangelicals have missed. The starting point is the cultivation of the leader's inner life via the practice of the disciplines. Then the leader is equipped to lead others to the same still waters and restoration of the soul that he or she has experienced.

24. Bruce Demarest, *Satisfy Your Soul* (Colorado Springs: NavPress, 2000), 136–37. I also recommend Demarest's *Soul Guide for the Pursuit of the Inner Life* (NavPress, 2002).

Enroll a Select Few with You

Every leader has the impulse to help others. You have chosen this life of following Jesus, his words, his works, his methods, his character. Then comes the time for you to bring others along to walk with you. It is best to find two others in order to provide you with some accountability, and the dynamic of three working together will require a more disciplined approach, which gives more transformational traction. The idea is that you will develop a relationship of trust and allow each other to speak into your lives.

After a period of a few months to a year you should be able to see how the relationship has deepened your walk with God and with each other. If you have something that is meaningful, then prayerfully consider widening the group by each of you choosing two others to duplicate your experience. Over a period of two years you could develop a core community of fifteen to twenty who have walked together. By now you have enough people in meaningful transformation that it should have done two things: (1) It should have been noticed by the people in the lives of those involved. Marriage partners, work associates, children, and friends should be commenting on the character changes they have seen. (2) It should have created enough interest in others that they would want to be involved. This is when you take it to its next logical step.

Teach It to Everyone

Introduce and explain the life to everyone in your community. Tell them the need for the life, the call to the life, the habits of the life, etc. This journey can be introduced in a church through a sermon series and/or a retreat. In a business or other secular associations, a retreat of the willing is best. Once you have a core community, they will provide the credibility needed in order to captivate others as well as being trained leaders in the principle of discipleship.

I introduced this concept in a nine-week sermon series called "Choose the Life." This was followed by another series on each of the spiritual disciplines. I also have used retreats—several one-day events called "Training Days" during which we developed the concepts in a more concrete way.

Society of the Willing

There is always a segment of any spiritual group who hunger for more. In my case 120 people chose the life and agreed to meet with others in order to go deeper with God, to break through the obedience barriers that had delayed their transformation. The main lesson we learned was that the higher we set the bar, the hungrier they became. Another major lesson was that what was supervised well flourished and what was supervised poorly failed. This goes back to one of the principles from one of my other works: You can't make disciples without accountability and you can't have accountability with large numbers without structure.

The society will flourish if it is *modeled* by the leaders, but it is also imperative that it be *managed* by the leaders. This does not take a great deal of work, but it needs to be clear and consistent. Most of the time it is best if the individuals select their own partners with whom to meet. If that is not possible, then those involved will need to be assessed as to their places along the journey. Then based on assessment they can be matched with others of common interest or relationship. A curriculum of books to read or studies to complete is helpful to provide some structure so they don't get lost in a directionless relationship. Someone should contact each group once a month to see how they are doing and if they need help.

The challenge is immense, but the pressure is off because when we enroll in this life with humility and in submission, we don't have to make anything happen. We simply must devote ourselves to live out the life Jesus lived, looking to God alone as our spiritual sustenance. We give up the gods that distracted and had such a hold on our lives. We give ourselves to the development of the inner life, give our best effort to the discipleship principle, and then give ourselves to others. In the end there will be a new order of societies throughout this land of men and women who have chosen the life. And those who have so chosen will be transformed and will transform those around them.

I leave you this prayer from Henri Nouwen:

Why do I keep relating to you as one of my many relationships, instead of my only relationship, in which all other ones are grounded? Why do I keep looking for popularity, respect from others, success, acclaim, and sensual pleasures? Why, Lord, is it so hard for me to make you the only one? Why do I keep hesitating to surrender myself totally to you?

Help me, O Lord, to let my old self die, to let die the thousand big and small ways in which I am still building up my false self and trying to cling to my false desires. Let me be reborn in you and see through you the world in the right way, so that all my actions, words, and thoughts can become a hymn of praise to you. I need your loving grace to travel on this hard road that leads to the death of my old self and to a new life in and for you. I know and trust that this is the road to freedom. Lord, dispel my mistrust and help me become a trusting friend. Amen.[25]

---

25. Henri J. M. Nouwen, *A Cry for Mercy: Prayers from the Genesee* (New York: Image Books, 2002).

Bill Hull's mission is to call the church to return to its disciple-making roots. He is a writer and discipleship evangelist calling the church to *choose the life* to which Jesus called every disciple—a life of spiritual transformation and service. A veteran pastor, Bill has written ten books on this subject. In 1990 he founded T-NET International, a ministry devoted to transforming churches into disciple-making churches.

The core of Bill's writing is *Jesus Christ, Disciplemaker*; *The Disciple-Making Pastor*; and *The Disciple-Making Church*. He now spends his time helping leaders experience personal transformation so they can help transform their churches. He also is involved in a project to form Choose the Life communities wherever there is need or interest.

Bill and his wife, Jane, have been married thirty-four years and are blessed to have two sons, a daughter-in-law, and a grandson. They live a not-so-quiet life in Long Beach, California.

For more information, go to www.BillHull.com.

ESSENTIAL RESOURCES *on* DISCIPLE MAKING

Jesus Christ, Disciplemaker
Updated Edition
0-8010-9169-1
$14.99, paperback

Jesus turned fishermen and tax collectors into some of the most influential men to ever live. You, too, can empower regular people to meet their potential as servants of God.

The standard resource in disciple making for over twenty years, *Jesus Christ, Disciplemaker* outlines Christ's methods in training his twelve disciples and shows you how to emulate Christ's model for reaching the lost.

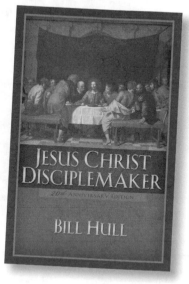

"This book deserves attention by anyone serious about making Christian disciples."—Robert Coleman, Gordon-Conwell Theological Seminary

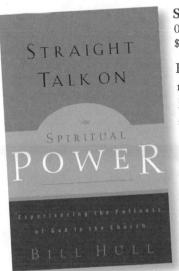

Straight Talk on Spiritual Power
0-8010-9136-5
$14.99, paperback

How can the church experience the fullness of God? What does it mean to move in the power of the Holy Spirit? Find answers to these questions and more with this balanced, scriptural look at the ministry of the Holy Spirit in the church today. Using personal stories and practical wisdom, Bill Hull carefully discusses sensitive topics, such as speaking in tongues, baptism with the Holy Spirit, healing, prophecy, and miracles.

B:BAKER | ww.bakerbooks.com

DISCIPLE MAKING
is for EVERY CHRISTIAN and EVERY CHURCH.

The Disciple-Making Pastor
0-8010-5720-3
$12.99, paperback

Bill Hull helps pastors reevaluate priorities and methods to become leaders who ignite their church members to be doers of the Word and not hearers only. He offers practical ways to transform believers who depend on the pastor for everything into disciples who go out and make more disciples. Once the momentum and direction have been established, amazing transformation will follow.

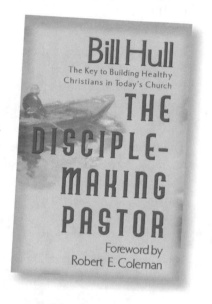

The Disciple-Making Church
0-8010-5627-4
$14.99, paperback

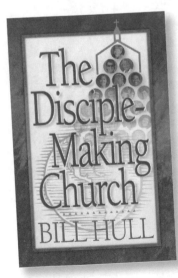

Everyone is called to make disciples of every nation. Bill Hull offers insight on how to make the disciple-making life a reality for every believer. Bringing the principles of the first-century church into our time, Hull calms fears and misconceptions about disciple making and empowers Christians to make their lives count for Christ.